Robert H. Lowie

Leaders of Modern Anthropology Series
Charles Wagley, GENERAL EDITOR

ROBERT H. LOWIE

by Robert F. Murphy

Columbia University Press
1972 NEW YORK AND LONDON

Copyright © 1972 Columbia University Press
Printed in the United States of America

Library of Congress Cataloging in Publication Data

Murphy, Robert Francis, 1924–
    Robert H. Lowie.

    (Leaders of modern anthropology series)
    Selected writings of Robert H. Lowie": pp. 77–175
    Bibliography: pp. 176–79
    1. Lowie, Robert Harry, 1883–1957 2. Ethnology.
      I. Lowie, Robert Harry, 1883–1957. II. Series.
GN21.L73M8   309.2'092'4 [B]   72–1969
ISBN 0-231-03375-3
ISBN 0-231-03397-4 (pbk.)

To Julian H. Steward, 1902-1972

Preface

✤ Robert H. Lowie (1883–1957) was one of the world's great anthropologists. Like many another great man, however, his contribution has not received the recognition that it merited, and he is best remembered today for having destroyed systems of theory rather than for building them. The critical character of his scholarship overshadowed the very important and constructive aspects of his writings, ideas which were too often forgotten, or reinvented years later by absent-minded students of the discipline. But Lowie deserves closer study, for a far more significant figure in anthropology's history emerges from a careful rereading of his work. Critical as he may have been, he was not negative. To the contrary, he was the embodiment of the very best of American anthropology in his time and one of the architects of the discipline that has evolved since then.

This volume is intended for the student of anthropology, but it is hoped that my professional colleagues will find sympathy with my re-evaluation of Lowie. Basically, the work is divided into two major parts: in the first, I examine Lowie's life and writings, and, in the second, six of his essays are reprinted as exemplars of his views and style. The first part, in turn, contains two sections. I begin with a

* Photograph courtesy of the Robert H. Lowie Museum of Anthropology at the University of California, Berkeley.

Preface

short professional biography of Lowie, based upon his own reminiscences, the recollections of his students, and my own memories of him, memories that are perhaps biased by my affection for the man and by the fact that I knew him only during the last two years of his life. In the second half of my essay on Lowie, his theories are analyzed and evaluated. Lowie wrote voluminously, and the task of choosing a limited number of his essays for presentation in this volume was most difficult. Some of his more technical works were avoided, and I sought also for variety of subject matter. But the selections can do no more than give a sample of his thought and an invitation to deeper study.

The book has profited from the help and guidance of many people. Professor Charles Wagley encouraged me to undertake the task and gave as critical a reading of the manuscript as he once did of my term papers. I am also grateful to Professor Cora Du Bois for her close reading of the book and for many valuable insights into Lowie and his times. Among the other students and associates of Robert Lowie, upon whose knowledge and memories I drew, I acknowledge with thanks Drs. Mary Haas, Margaret Lantis, Harry Shapiro, Julian H. Steward, and Bella Weitzner. Finally, Drs. William Bascom and Edward Norbeck were so kind as to provide photographs of Lowie, and Mrs. Jessie Malinowska gave her utmost care to the preparation of the manuscript.

It is customary at this juncture to offer thanks to the university or foundation that provided the free time for writing, but I had no free time. Rather, I should acknowledge my debt to an academic departmental chairmanship, from which misery writing has been for the last three years my principal escape. It may be noted that Lowie too wrote a great deal during such inauspicious periods.

New York City   Robert F. Murphy
January 1972

Contents

✣ PART I
ROBERT H. LOWIE: A REMINISCENCE 1
Lowie the Ethnographer 8
Lowie the Social Theorist 43

✣ PART II
SELECTED WRITINGS OF ROBERT H. LOWIE 77

*Reminiscences of Anthropological Currents
   in America Half a Century Ago* 78
Social Organization 109
*Exogamy and the Classificatory System
   of Relationship* 124
The Territorial Tie 129
*Property Rights and Coercive Powers of Plains
   Indian Military Societies* 144
Religion in Human Life 159

BIBLIOGRAPHY 176

Robert H. Lowie

PART I

Robert H. Lowie

ROBERT H. LOWIE: A REMINISCENCE

Robert Harry Lowie was a punctual man. He invariably entered his seminar room just before the appointed hour, never late but never early either. There lies a key to the man in this trivial fact. Lowie epitomized form, propriety, decorum, and punctility in his public role as a professor; he would find lateness an affront if committed by a student but an abomination if committed by himself. The students were well aware of this and were always assembled before Lowie would make his entrance, stand before them beaming benignly, and begin the session with a slight bow, saying "Good afternoon, gentlemen." Nobody stood up as he entered, as was done in the older Continental tradition, but there was always a stirring as the students drew more erect in their seats. Lowie, in turn, knew the students well and, to avoid either inconveniencing them by impelling them to earlier arrival or embarrassing them by entering the room before them, he took care to arrive exactly on time. Always a very careful man in the perilous area of social relationships, he was most aware of his own behavior as a form of ceremonial performance.

This blend of formality and protocol on the one hand and sensitivity and consideration for his students on the other was neither contradiction nor paradox. Lowie was formal because form conferred predictability, and predictability is a virtue in the old when dealing with the young. If he appeared stuffy and pompous to his students —as he often did—he did so while avoiding arbitrariness and capriciousness, and thereby remained evenhanded and just. He was a stern master and threw his graduate students into panic with staggering reading lists. But they knew that hard work was exactly, and only, what he expected of them, and was the common ground on which he would meet them as fellow anthropologists. For the student who met Lowie's standards for the working scholar, he was totally accessible and open, absolutely absorbed in the student's research and wholly receptive to ideas. Behind the forbidding aspect of the Germanic professor was a kind and shy man, totally committed to his discipline and his students, strictly observant of a hierarchy of manners, but equally dedicated to egalitarianism in the realm of thought.

When I first arrived at the University of California's Berkeley campus in 1955 as an assistant professor in his first teaching post, I was filled with the usual anxieties and migivings. The eminence of the Berkeley campus was sufficiently awesome, but for an anthropologist the department was also something of an ancestral cult center, harboring as it still did its very active emeritus professors, Robert Harry Lowie and Alfred Louis Kroeber. Both were *eminences grises* in the grand style. Each was a Huxley Medalist, a Viking Medalist, a member of the National Academy of Sciences, among a long roster of honors. Most anthropologists at the time would probably have accorded Kroeber the distinction of being "the greatest living anthropologist," but Lowie would have had many protagonists; there would have been no other contestants.

I had known Kroeber from the years in which he taught at Columbia, where I had done my graduate study, but my first encounter with Robert Lowie, except for distant glimpses at professional gatherings, was at Berkeley. I first approached him with some trepidation, for he had a reputation as something of a martinet, a stuffy and aloof person who seemingly would hold little sympathy for the ecologically oriented anthropology that I had learned at Columbia. Lowie put me at ease immediately, however, by turning our conversations to our common interests. He listened avidly to every detail of the culture of the Brazilian Mundurucú, a group I had recently studied, and he regaled me with mountains of comparative information on Brazilian Indians. It became clear that Lowie was doing vicarious field work through me. Although he had had a consuming interest in South American Indians ever since his association in the 1930s with Kurt Nimuendajú, a German ethnographer noted for his studies of the Gê peoples of Brazil, he had never done actual research there. His knowledge of the continent was nonetheless voluminous, as it was for the ethnography of most other parts of the world. We also shared an interest in the Shoshone Indians, studied by Lowie in 1906 and by myself a half-century later. Despite the time lapse, he had a remarkable recall for events and people. With eyes half closed he would lean back in his chair and conjure up for his listener the jarring of the stage coach as it wound across the Continental Divide into the Lemhi Valley, and tell of the lost days of the early West in that remote and isolated pocket of the Rocky Mountains.

I always assumed the role of student toward Lowie, out of sheer inability to do otherwise, but he in turn treated me as a colleague, although always as a junior one. None of the junior faculty members could quite bring themselves to call him "Bob" or even "Robert," but Lowie recognized the deference pattern and never pushed himself into a first-name basis with younger people. He seemed to understand familiarity as a form of intrusion, an invasion of privacy. Distance, then, was correspondingly a form of self-protection and a basis of good relationships. This is good sociology, and Lowie followed out its premises by always addressing his junior associates with the "doctor" title. It was all very Old World and gracious—perhaps stilted by current standards, but perfectly proper and expectable with Lowie.

In keeping with his willingness to meet younger anthropologists

Robert H. Lowie

as fellow scholars, he was always a gentle critic of our theories, however much they may have differed from his own views. I had expected a snort at my ecological interests, but he listened to them carefully and tried to help me sharpen my ideas. In time I came to see that, despite Lowie's well-known lack of interest in environment and economy, my own ecological perspectives had been influenced by Julian H. Steward, who had, in turn, been a graduate student of Lowie's. He knew exactly what I was talking about and was not so much hostile to Steward's cultural ecology as simply concerned with other things. In fact, Lowie had a profound influence on Steward's treatment of social organization, which is a central part of his cultural ecological method. In his later writings, Lowie occasionally berated himself for not having given technology and livelihood their due, for nobody was more aware than he that the major shortcoming of his ethnographic description of the Crow Indians was exactly this.

Despite his essential kindliness to graduate students, most of those I knew at Berkeley regarded Lowie with an awe that approached fright. He was a large-proportioned and portly man, bald and with ample jowls, his face dominated by severe steel-rimmed glasses and a close-cropped mustache. His appearance fitted his reserve completely, and both, combined with a reputation for exacting standards, were most formidable. He believed that fluency, or at least facility, in German was one of the hallmarks of the scholar, and routinely failed most of the graduate students who took the German reading proficiency examination. The students were also convinced that one Lowie seminar was equal to a full course load, which was close to the truth. Lowie saw no reason why a student should not read almost everything ever written on the Sun Dance of the Plains Indians in one week; and when he sent his seminar off to read Alexander Goldenweiser, he expected them to *know* Goldenweiser. As a faithful attendant at both the seminars that Lowie gave from 1955 to 1957, I developed a facility for sitting very quietly and looking wise. When Lowie asked my opinion of a book or article, I would usually be stumped and have to turn the question. I doubt whether it fooled him, for he very considerately stopped querying me. But apprehension about Lowie was always most acute among those students who knew him least. The others came to know his shyness, and they also came to know that he was concerned that they have a good opinion of his scholarship.

For all his fame and reputation, Lowie was deeply uncertain of the quality of some of his most widely acclaimed works. He has written that his best-known book, *Primitive Society*, received plaudits only because it was the first survey of primitive social organization since the decline of nineteenth-century theories of cultural evolution. Lowie thought that it had some good points, but that it was hastily written and premature. This self-doubt joined with the aloof dignity of the German scholar to make Lowie somewhat defensive in seminar. What resulted was a curious interaction in which both professor and students were afraid that they would be found wanting. He gave a seminar on his own work which was at once wonderfully frank and acutely ambivalent about the subject matter. But, in the final analysis, Lowie on Lowie turned out to deal more directly with his contemporaries of his younger days at Columbia and the American Museum of Natural History, and the seminar turned into a fascinating and personal narrative of the early years of American anthropology.

Lowie's seminar on Lowie and his contemporaries revealed one of his more remarkable qualities, a memory that was tenacious, detailed, and rich with imagery. He told his audience at one session that he had taken statistics with Professor Franz Boas at Columbia in the spring term of 1905. At the next meeting he appeared before the group in some embarrassment for having misled them on the date, which was really the fall semester of 1904. Lowie asked that allowance be made for the memory of a man of his years; unable to trust his failing mnemonic powers, he had checked his old Columbia registration cards. The differences of time had no significance for Lowie's education, let alone the history of anthropology. But facts were facts, and accuracy of reporting transcended the context and purposes of the report. Indeed, to Lowie the larger picture was absolutely founded upon a myriad of accurate factual material and emanated directly from such data. On another occasion, Lowie was in a nostalgic mood, and recalled the evening when he and a few other young students of Franz Boas were guests of Elsie Clews Parsons. Elsie Parsons was one of Boas's first students, and she went on to acquire a lasting reputation for her ethnography of Puebloan and Middle American Indians. She was also a person of considerable wealth, and her door was always open to the impecunious graduate students of her day. Lowie recalled the dinner served at the Parsons home one evening almost a half-century earlier with gusto and epicurean detail, and then said: "We went on to Dr. Parsons's box at the opera that night and saw. . . ." His memory had failed him, the second time that this had happened in the time I knew him. Many of his students had a hard time remembering what they had eaten the night before or the courses they had taken the previous semester, leaving them more smitten with a sense of their own weak memories than by Lowie's lapse.

The fantastic wealth of data in Lowie's mind was both a source and a result of his approach to anthropology. We will cover his theories in detail, but it should be said now that he had at his command an encyclopedic knowledge of ethnography, as well as an impressive store of facts on almost everything. Lowie has been widely known as a "historical particularist," which means simply that he was very critical of theories that saw broad patterns in culture and that he was prone to view cultures as products of their particular histories rather than as an outcome of causes of a more general nature. For every generalization offered, he could think of at least one exception, and he sometimes dredged up a sufficient number to forever cloud the status of some statement as a social "law." There are many reasons for this hypercritical aspect of Lowie's thought, but it was certainly dependent upon a memory that could retain large quantities of isolated bits of information, as does a computer, and retrieve them in association with other information relevant to the problem at hand. Most people remember only what they consider important facts, but for Lowie every fact was important. He could prove this by drawing from his vast reservoir an armada of facts that laid waste entire realms of what he considered to be bad thinking.

Lowie could not abide scholarship that went beyond its data.

A Reminiscence

Science was empiricism and empiricism was science. Theories were built upon facts; facts were not fed into theories. And if he remembered everything, from Elsie Clews Parsons's menu to the clan names of the Zuni, it was as much a part of his science as a component of his personality. His standards of scientific proof were rigorous, as we shall see, and he could be very sharp with those who did not conform to them. This, and what some thought to be a quite negative approach to theory, gave him a reputation as a tough critic, even a bit of a tartar. Lowie had also absorbed much of the style of Continental, especially German, scholarship, which was noted for the vehemence of its disputes and a tradition of rich polemical writing. He sometimes expressed his various disagreements as polite demurrers, but when he found himself in fundamental opposition to another anthropologist's views he frequently took the aggressive— as he did when he disagreed with Professor Leslie White.

White had revived the nineteenth-century evolutionary theories of Lewis Henry Morgan in the 1940s, although Lowie had nearly buried them in 1920. This whole matter will be considered later in an account of Lowie's anthropology, but here we are concerned with the man and the wonderful climax of his argument with White, which revealed so much about both men. Lowie responded almost immediately to the resurrection of Morgan by White, and the dispute peppered the pages of anthropological journals in the late 1940s. Both were gifted debaters, and the articles displayed a great penchant for the barbed remark and the withering phrase. In one of these polemical pieces, Lowie commented: "I do not, however, impugn White's good faith; the obsessive power of fanaticism unconsciously warps one's vision (Lowie 1946:224)." There seemed little more that one could say.

In the light of this background, there was considerable speculation and uncertainty at Berkeley when Leslie White arrived for a term as Visiting Professor in the spring of 1956. The two men had conducted their argument in print, and they had never had more than a passing acquaintance with each other. In fact, White said at the time that one of his reasons for visiting Berkeley was to get to know Lowie. This he did, for, much to everybody's relief, Lowie and White were frequently seen in deep and cordial conversation with each other. One day White remarked to me that his Berkeley stay would always be a source of satisfaction if only because he had gotten to know what a splendid person Lowie really was. He added, in puzzlement, that it was hard to understand how Lowie could have written such diatribes against him. Some days later I saw Lowie, who told me that it was gratifying to learn that Leslie White was a truly charming gentleman, a fact that was hard to reconcile with some of his writing. Each was correct in his final appraisal of the other, but their contentiousness arose from a trait shared by both: Lowie was—and White remains—totally committed to anthropology as a discipline of the mind and as a way of life, and their strong adherence to their respective views was a function of this common faith.

Lowie mellowed in his later years, and his occasional scholarly pugnaciousness waned in the process. As he saw his anthropological career draw to a close, he placed his accomplishments in the perspective of work done and never to be repeated, standing as a fact that, like other facts, could be objectified and evaluated. This was a time in which the essential Viennese that underlay his formal exterior came out in all its gentleness and skepticism. He grew fond of looking back at his career with some bemusement and wonder at his own naïveté and shortcomings. One day he told his seminar on Lowie of his first field trip to the Shoshone. He seemed to drift away from us in time as he reminisced but, then, regaining awareness of his audience, he said: "I knew so little of anthropology when I started out. You gentlemen are ever so much better trained." It was exactly the right thing to have said.

LOWIE THE ETHNOGRAPHER   Elderly gentlemen have a penchant for reminiscence, but few have attracted such delighted audiences as did Lowie. He liked to talk about himself and well understood his role as witness to his discipline and to the people he studied. This led to the writing of an autobiography of his professional life, *Robert H. Lowie, Ethnol-*

ogist, which was published in 1959, two years after his death. The work reveals Lowie's shyness and restraint, but it subtly tells us more about him than would a frank confession. It is required reading for those wishing to gain an understanding of Lowie, and the primary source for the brief biography that follows.

Robert Harry Lowie was born in Vienna on June 12, 1883, the son of Samuel Lowie and Ernestine Kuhn Lowie. His father was a businessman, evidently not a very successful one, who was born in Budapest and had settled in the capital city of the old Austro-Hungarian Empire. Lowie's mother was a native-born Viennese, the daughter of a physician who specialized in diseases of the nose and throat and who was also a devotee of classical scholarship and of Goethe. The Lowie family was exemplary of the Austrian middle-class intelligentsia of the day, and much of Lowie's style and character must be understood in light of this. Although he spent all but ten years of his life in the United States, his Americanization was never complete.

If Lowie remained the product of a city which he left when only ten years old, it is partially because of strong family ties. One need not venture far into the temptations of analytic biography to suggest that his attachment to his mother and sister were of paramount importance to the young Lowie. He described his father as an observant, retiring, and quiet man whose muted character he attributed to economic reverses. He remembered his mother, however, as an outgoing and vibrant person of commanding appearance and presence, gifted in music and possessed of fine social graces. One senses that it was the mother who was the focal point of family life and the predominant influence in stimulating Lowie's intellectual interests. The Lowies had two surviving children, Robert and his younger sister Risa. Risa taught English in the high schools of New York City, and Lowie appreciated her as a fine poet with an extraordinary understanding of the views of others. Their attachment was life-long and deep.

Lowie entered the *Cherninschule* in Vienna in 1888, but at about the time when he was to enter the classical gymnasium the family emigrated to New York City. He entered Public School 83 on the Upper East Side, went through the city school system, and entered the City College of New York, from which he received the B.A. degree in 1901. Lowie's graduation from college at the age of eighteen, only eight years after coming to the United States, suggests precocity and industry as well as intelligence. It should be added that he first appeared in print when he was fifteen with an article on Edgar Allan Poe in the old *New Yorker Review* (Lowie, 1898).

It is well to remember that Lowie did not grow up in the United States as such, but specifically in New York City. His family resided in neighborhoods populated largely by German speakers, and lived its social life among persons having the same background in German culture. The New York Germans of Lowie's group were of a special breed. They included families which, like Lowie's, had some degree of Jewish background, although they had become quite alienated from their religious heritage and assimilated with German or German-Austrian culture. They were also educated and rationalistic in the older sense of being "free-thinkers," and their dedication to learning, political liberalism, and professional attainment was their only devotion. Lowie remarked that the great American "melting pot" was not doing very much melting in his neighborhoods or in his schools, up to and including college. He always felt himself to be a "marginal man." His German remained idiomatic and flawless, just as his English became impeccable and accentless, and to the end of his life he even dreamed in both languages. When very young, he was a founder of the *Deutscher Literarischer Verein*, and later he taught German in night school.

Lowie was evidently a superior student at City College, for he received the Claflin Medal in Greek and was elected to Phi Beta Kappa. After his graduation, with a degree in Classics, he taught in the city schools. But his friends had convinced him that science was the only worthwhile venture, which lead him to read widely in the general sciences and to take two summer courses in chemistry at Columbia. Convinced by his own manual ineptitude and by his interest only in the philosophical questions raised by science that he was not born to be a chemist, he drifted toward biological and

The Ethnographer

psychological interests. What attracted Lowie, and most other anthropologists, to anthropology is not clear, for he had had no prior training, and apparently little reading background, in the fledgling subject before entering graduate school. He wrote that he had been more impressed by a short sketch of Professor Franz Boas's qualifications that had appeared in a Columbia bulletin than by the subject itself. Boas's own training had been in the natural sciences and geography, and he brought to anthropology a scientific rigor and an empiricism that derived from his own training in Germany, and in the tradition of pure empiricism that is associated with the theories of Ernest Haeckel and Ernst Mach. These nineteenth-century scientists had also been among the most important early influences upon Lowie; his cultural and intellectual roots entwined with those of Boas. Perhaps, also, Lowie was motivated into anthropology by the German translations of Cooper's *Leatherstocking Tales* which he remembered so vividly. Whatever the reason, he entered Columbia in 1904.

The discipline, and the university, that Lowie entered was a different world entirely from today's anthropology, and Columbia University now. Boas had arrived there as recently as 1896, after teaching from 1889 to 1892 at Clark University and spending the next two years preparing exhibits at the Chicago World's Fair. The department soon became centered completely upon Boas, although Livingston Farrand took some part in the teaching program. Very few students were enrolled in anthropology during these early years, and academic life was close and intense. There was a great deal to be done in anthropology, few people to do it, and the students were drawn precipitously into the work of the profession. The roster of Boas's early students is indicative of both the sparseness of their numbers and his great achievement as a teacher. From 1901 to 1911, the following people received their degrees from Columbia: Alfred L. Kroeber, William Jones, Albert B. Lewis, Robert H. Lowie, Edward Sapir, Alexander Goldenweiser, and Paul Radin. The profession at that time could hold its annual convention in one small meeting room. Today the conventions require the facilities of large metropolitan hotels. It was a heady period for the new discipline.

Robert H. Lowie

People barely knew what an anthropologist was, and nobody seemed to have any clear ideas about how a Ph.D. program in the subject should be planned. Boas's method seemed to be that of sink or swim. He put his students to work on anthropological research, and if they did it well they received a degree. Today we seem to be coming back to the same system.

In his autobiography, Lowie confesses to a largely wasted first year at Columbia. Most of the courses were completely over his head. He took statistical theory with Boas and was lost, and nothing in his prior education had prepared him for Boas's advanced seminar on American Indian languages. To round things off, he took a course with Adolphe Bandelier on Spanish sources for Latin American research; and since he knew little about Latin America, a knowledge of bibliographic resources seemed only to compound his ignorance. He somehow survived the first year of graduate study, with the help of Livingston Farrand and Clark Wissler, who had just been appointed to the chairmanship of the Department of Anthropology at the American Museum of Natural History. Although registered for the doctoral program in anthropology, Lowie also took a minor in psychology. Most of his work in that field was with Columbia's two great turn-of-the-century psychologists, James McKeen Cattell and Robert S. Woodworth. Lowie, however, could never be identified with the group of scholars, which included Edward Sapir and Margaret Mead, who introduced psychological concerns into anthropology. But his lifelong preoccupation with the field shows up clearly in his writings on religion, although he never became known for having much psychological prescience.

In a revealing passage, Lowie wrote: "No ethnologist—not even Boas—was ever my hero or my source of inspiration" (1959:170). This is true to a greater extent than most anthropologists realize, and to call Lowie a "Boasian" is a great oversimplification of both Lowie and Boas. Both men, as we have noted, were steeped in the nonspeculative, nonmetaphysical, and highly descriptive orientation of German science at that time, and the unwillingness of both to generalize broadly or to engage in theorization that went beyond the immediate facts at hand was part of this larger tradition. It is interesting that although the German sociologists Max Weber and Georg Simmel were both alive during Lowie's early career, neither shared this narrow empiricism, and apparently had little influence upon him. Indeed, Lowie confessed that he never read sociology for pleasure, but preferred works in the philosophy of science. Lowie's anthropology emerged from his attempt to make the field a science and subject to all the rules of evidence and canons of proof that one would find in physics. That his science never achieved the results of physics was due not to lack of rigor on his part but to the vagaries of the human situation. Today, few anthropologists feel constrained to emulate the pure sciences, and those who do are operating in a more flexible and open scientific atmosphere in which hypothesis and conjecture are once again respectable. Lowie saw this shift in his later years, and, although his admiration for Haeckel and Mach remained undiminished, his ideas became more venturesome.

What Lowie derived from Boas was largely his caution, skepticism, and love for facts. But, since this general tenor of thought was characteristic of most anthropologists in the early part of the century, we cannot describe the man only as a disciple of Boas, strong though the tie was. He actually spoke little of Franz Boas in his seminars, and the persons he mentioned most often as specific influences were such of his contemporaries as Alexander Goldenweiser, Paul Radin, Elsie Clews Parsons, Alfred Kroeber, Leslie Spier, and others. The most important of his teachers in anthropology proper was probably Clark Wissler, who sent Lowie off on his first field trip to the Shoshone and guided his early research on North American Indians. Lowie's Ph.D. dissertation was, however, written under Boas and was largely based on research in existing sources. The thesis, entitled "The Test-Theme in North American Mythology," and published in the *Journal of American Folklore* (1908), was Lowie's first venture into the analysis of myths and folktales. He received the Ph.D. in 1908, only four years after entering graduate school, which is rapid by today's standards. Since he spent a good deal of this time in field work, and had entered anthropology with only an inkling of what the subject was about, one can understand

Robert H. Lowie

Lowie's own later misgivings about his training. However, the discipline was new as a profession at the time, and even its students were engaged less in learning a body of received wisdom than in creating one.

Lowie had begun to work as a volunteer assistant to Wissler in the American Museum of Natural History while still a graduate student, and it was Wissler who arranged for Lowie's work in 1906 among the Shoshone of the Lemhi Reservation in Idaho. The Shoshone Indians are less a "tribe" in any political sense of the term than a population speaking mutually intelligible dialects of the Shoshone language and having many similarities of custom. They are one branch of the Uto-Aztecan linguistic family, which includes such diverse groups as the Aztecans of Mexico, the pueblo-dwelling Hopi of Arizona, the Comanche, the Ute, and the Northern Paiute, to name only the principal branches. The Shoshone proper occupied a vast territory between the Rockies and the Sierra Nevadas. All were hunters and gatherers, and their small groups were found scattered from southern California northward through the Great Basin into central Idaho, and on an east-west axis from central Nevada through northern Utah into central Wyoming. Although Lowie speaks of the particular group he visited as "Lemhi Shoshone," "Lemhi Indians," or just plain "Lemhis," the only sociological referent of the term is to the fact that much of the Shoshone population of the mountains north of the Snake River plain had been settled at the Mormon town of Lemhi, Idaho. Shortly after Lowie's visit they were resettled on the Fort Hall Reservation, near the city of Pocatello, Idaho.

Practically nothing was known of the Shoshone in 1906, a point that Lowie stresses in his autobiography. Most of the information available at the times came from the journals of explorers and fur trappers, such as Lewis and Clark, John Fremont, Alexander Ross, and Jedediah Smith. Even these accounts were fragmentary, for few travelers thought the Shoshone to be worthy of much attention, living as they did at the margin of survival and having a very simple culture. And to compound Lowie's problem, almost nothing was known of the Shoshone of the area in which he was to work. Given

The Ethnographer

the fact that our general knowledge of North American ethnography, or cultural descriptions, was little better off at the time, one can only wonder why Wissler bothered to send Lowie to study the Shoshone at all. The probable answer is that Wissler needed some Shoshone ethnography to back up his own work on the neighboring Blackfoot, for most of Lowie's early researches were on groups girdling the Blackfoot country.

Lowie's account of his first meeting with the Shoshone is a classic of its kind, for he describes all of the bumbling mistakes and disappointments of the student, fresh from graduate school, in his first encounter with "his people." Reading it brought back to mind my own experience of what I felt to be a historic first encounter with Brazilian Indians. My wife and I had been traveling up the Tapajós River toward the country of the Mundurucú Indians for two weeks. One day a trader announced that some Mundurucú were living temporarily at his store. We braced ourselves for the great moment of confrontation, which came when three Mundurucú women, dressed in Mother Hubbard dresses, approached us, took one look, broke into uncontrollable laughter, and ran away. Lowie's big moment was similarly anticlimactic. Stopping off at Fort Hall enroute to Lemhi, he met his first Shoshone, from whom he immediately and directly tried to extract information. His informants either remained mute or made fun of him, and he had no success until he was able to talk to an old lady in privacy.

Given the state of knowledge about North American Indians, the Shoshone trip could hardly have been a failure, but neither, then, was it a great success. As every reservation ethnographer knows, Indians do not necessarily welcome their questions, and the general distrust of whites carries over into the field work situation. This reticence can sometimes be overcome by prolonged residence, but Lowie had only two-and-a-half months at his disposal. Another problem was that simply of trying to find the people. This is difficult enough where an automobile is available, but Lowie had to learn to ride a horse, no mean feat for a young man raised in Vienna and New York City. The final problem was the simple one of communication, for at that time very few Shoshone spoke English, and Lowie knew no Shoshone. He found one bilingual man on the entire reservation, but he would not work for the paltry wages allowed by Lowie's stipend. The erstwhile ethnographer then tried to find interpreters from among the students at the Indian day school, but he soon discovered that the schools did a poor job of teaching English. It could be added that young boys are hardly effective interpreters when working with older informants for the obvious reason of the relative statuses of the old and young. And Lowie, in accord with ethnographic method at that time, had to work with older men.

Under such circumstances, the ethnographer can always settle down and simply watch what people do. But Lowie notes that there was not much worth watching. Most of the Indians lived in cabins, the native artifacts had been largely replaced by manufactured articles, and the aboriginal economy had been totally and finally ended by reservation life. Of course, it could be argued that anything that a group of people do is intrinsically worth recording and is a proper subject of ethnography, but one must consider the aims of American anthropology in the early twentieth century. First, as Lowie tells us, the ways of life of American peoples were not adequately recorded, and the primary goal of research was to complete the description. Anthropologists quite rightly did not go out to study one "problem" or another or to test hypotheses; they were working in the early period of their researches, using the methods of description and classification of the natural sciences. Linnaeus had to precede microbiology, and even Darwin; Lowie's Shoshone research had to precede that of his students Julian H. Steward and Dmitri Shimkin. And just what facts should be gathered was dictated by the situation of the American Indian.

It was clear to any intelligent person of the period that American Indian culture was moribund. The remaining Indians, only a fraction of their former numbers, had been herded onto reservations, and whites had occupied most of their lands. The Shoshone were actually fortunate in having been placed on reservations within their former habitat; other groups had been transported over a thousand miles to the Indian Territory of Oklahoma. Most of the

The Ethnographer

reservation Indians were reduced to dependency upon the government for rations. Robbed of their lands and deprived of their autonomy, they were further reduced to despondency. Desultory attempts were made by the government to induce the Shoshone to farm, but they were traditionally hunters, and their own lack of inclination to till the soil combined with the fact that most of it was untillable. They still continued to do a bit of hunting and collecting of wild roots, seeds, and berries, but for the most part there was little to do but engage in occasional wage labor or just sit around. Without its economic base, as Lowie well understood (Lowie, 1959:68), the culture of the Shoshone, and those of the rest of the American Indians, was rapidly dying. The ethnographer's task was to salvage a record of what was left before it disappeared.

"Salvage ethnography," as it is called, produced a distinctive kind of field work, which inevitably became reflected in theory. Indeed, it can be argued that Lowie's theories were much more a result of his work with American Indians than of his study under Franz Boas, although it was Boas who impressed upon his students the importance of salvage ethnography. American anthropology set as its task the recording of the indigenous cultures, the way of life that existed before the coming of the whites, rather than the reservation life that was the reality of the Indian. There was precious little left to observe, although there was probably more than most students at the time realized. To be sure, the externals, the exoterica, of native cultures were attenuated, but one could still observe a few of the old economic activities. More important, patterns of family life and the nuances of social interaction had not been altered as much as other aspects of culture, and one could record how an Indian mother raised her children, what was proper social conduct, how people positioned their bodies and manipulated expression, and countless other things. But these were not the main institutional attributes of Indian society, and the ethnographer interested in economy, political organization, religion, and larger kinship groupings had to rely largely on the memories of informants.

At the time of Lowie's visit to Lemhi, the Indians had already been on reservation for some thirty years, so he had to depend upon the recollections of rather old informants. There thus emerged the field method of finding the oldest persons, generally males and hopefully articulate ones, and, so to speak, pumping them dry. The common yield of this procedure was normative information; that is, data on the rules and values that regulated social life. It was more difficult to find out who did what, when, where, and with whom—the standard questions of all social anthropologists—because situational material, recollections of actual events, were harder to come by. The material also underwent transformation in being converted from perception to experience and thence from experience to memory. And what do most mature persons remember? They remember those things that they cherish or which excited their fancies, which is human enough, but not a very good sieve for objective reality. Golden times in which the world was simpler and things happened according to plan and expectation are recalled. Memory produces order, and the picture of Indian life that developed with salvage ethnography was that of a pristine and changeless time when unity prevailed.

Memory is uncertain and treacherous, and what is recalled comes out in neatly objectified pieces, reduced to simplicity and order. These were the units of data that anthropology dealt with in those days. Or perhaps we should say that the mode of collection accounted for the data. The anthropologists of the time were students of custom, of putatively discrete and unitary culture traits that could be delimited, catalogued, and classified. They collected a wealth of symbolic material, most of which was divorced from behavior; the culture was remembered and not acted out. One also receives a sense of cultural homogeneity from the early monographs that was only occasionally relieved by warnings that there was disagreement between informants. The ethnographer might ask: "Was it considered good in those times to marry your cross-cousin?" If he received two or three affirmative responses, the group was irrevocably listed as practicing cross-cousin marriage. One could not know with what frequency and remained uncertain about informant reliability on whether either cross-cousin was acceptable. The tendency to work with a limited number of old informants sometimes resulted

The Ethnographer

in ethnographies based on the recollections of only one man. Lowie, it should be stressed, never did this. But even when a number of informants agreed on a point, the investigator might well wonder whether this homogeneity was the result, among old reservation residents, of a strain toward agreement of oral traditions. Ideas tend toward a certain neatness when they are not being continually torn apart by the realities of human actions.

My pointing to the pitfalls of these procedures is not meant as criticism, for the reservation ethnographers were narrowly circumscribed by the limits imposed by the situation of the American Indian. Lowie had, as has been said, a passion for factual accuracy, and he always tried to corroborate his information with as many informants as possible. And he observed what could still be seen. Still, he did not see the ethnographer's task to be one of total immersement and full participant observation. When he arrived in Lemhi, Lowie was given quarters by the Indian Agent, which lead him in his autobiography to enter the rather defensive note that he had indeed camped with Indians, though not frequently. He simply did not see living among the Indians as a necessity or even as a possibility. He relied heavily, almost completely, upon interviews, and these are generally best conducted in privacy and away from interested, sometimes censorious, spectators. It could be added that modern ethnographers, like Lowie before them, quite commonly look after their own creature comforts, and some of the finest examples of complete participant observation result from field situations that came about only because no other quarters were available. In any event, anybody who knew Lowie could hardly imagine him living easily in the ambience of an Indian household.

Lowie, as he put it, "won his spurs" among the Shoshone but he accomplished a few other things as well. He had initiated a lifelong interest in mythology and folklore, and ultimately primitive religion, actually collecting enough data in one summer for a short monograph on the Northern Shoshone (Lowie 1909a) and an article on folklore (Lowie and St. Claire 1909). This is more than most students produce from a summer's field work even in our, in theory, more advanced system of training. And, as he always told his seminars, he

Robert H. Lowie

had done research among an aboriginal North American group without clans, contrary to Lewis Henry Morgan's thesis in *Ancient Society* (1877) that clanship was general to the evolutionary stage represented by the American Indian.

In 1907, the year before he received his Ph.D. degree, Lowie was appointed to the post of Assistant in the American Museum of Natural History; he was promoted to Assistant Curator in 1909 and to Associate Curator in 1912. His association with Wissler thus became formalized into a working relationship that was to last fourteen years. Lowie was eclipsed by Wissler at the Museum, just as he was later by Kroeber at Berkeley, but in both cases the secondary position was due less to relative accomplishments than to the mildness and self-effacement that were integral to Lowie's personality. The Museum position proved to be ideal for the advancement of Lowie's ethnological career, for it was during this period that the bulk of his field work was carried out. Today, most ethnographic research is done by scholars holding university teaching posts, but in Lowie's early years the great museums were equally, and probably more, important sources of field workers. There are two reasons for this. The first, and simpler, is that the universities have grown faster than the museums. The second is that, while museum personnel were expected to be out doing research and collecting artifacts as part of their normal duties, it took the universities a long time to come around to this point of view. A professor was paid to teach, and teach he did. Sabbatical leaves were not yet part of the perquisites of life in most universities, and funds from outside agencies were either severely limited or nonexistent. In retrospect, it is amazing that the anthropologists of a half century ago were able to accomplish the amount of research they actually did, which was enormous. Part of the answer lies in the fact that they carried on summer programs with munificent budgets of two or three hundred dollars, plus some of their own meager funds. They were dedicated men.

After Lowie joined the faculty at Berkeley in 1921, his field work was restricted to a visit to the Washo of Nevada and California, in 1926, and his last trip to the Crow Indians of Montana in 1931. Retirement freed him for a six-month study of German culture in

The Ethnographer

1950, but the last half of his life was otherwise taken up by writing and teaching. Thus, by the time Lowie had reached his mid-thirties he had already completed the corpus of his life's field research. His museum career happily coincided with his anthropological youth, which, after all, is the time when most anthropologists do their best empirical research. This is the time when one has the psychological resiliency to cope with the vagaries of life in different cultures; and it is also the period when one has the physical stamina so commonly required in ethnography. Today, when most Indian reservations can be reached in hours by jet plane and rented car, this is of less importance, but western North America in Lowie's day was only a few decades removed from the frontier, and much of it was still raw, wild, and beautiful.

Many persons think of Lowie as having devoted himself almost exclusively to the Crow, for this was the group that he knew best and had studied most thoroughly; it was also the one with which he formed a lasting personal identification as an ethnographer. He actually, however, did fieldwork among more American Indian groups than most other anthropologists of his time, or since then. In addition to the Crow and Northern Shoshone, he spent varying amounts of time with the Assiniboine, Northern Blackfoot and Chipewyans of Alberta, the Hidatsa in North Dakota, the Southern Ute of Colorado, the Southern Paiute of Nevada and Utah, the Northern Paiute, or Paviotso, of western Nevada, the Washo of Nevada and California, and the Hopi of Arizona. In the process, Lowie acquired a reputation as an occasional student of the Southwest, a knowledgeable specialist on the Great Basin and the world's foremost authority on Plains Indians.

As part of his apprenticeship under Wissler, Lowie was sent in the spring of 1907 on an ethnographic tour of the northern high plains. Characteristically, his work took him to the Northern Blackfoot of Alberta and to the peripheries of the Blackfoot country. Wissler gave Lowie marching orders in the style of the military. He was sent to the Blackfoot specifically and only to take down a single myth in their native language, and was directed to proceed afterward for a brief stop at the Cree and thence to the Assiniboine of the Stony reservation, also in Alberta. Upon completing his work there, he was instructed to remain until he received further orders!

Lowie found the Blackfoot camped out at the railroad station in Gleichen, Alberta, their tepees arranged in the classic Plains circle. Although the occasion for this festive gathering was the birthday of King Edward VII, Lowie found the camp to be the nearest approximation to native Plains life that he was to see. The Indians, however, were in a particularly antagonistic mood toward the whites, and Lowie had to devise a way of gaining their interest and finding an interpreter. He did this by walking through the camp making "cat's cradles," the string games that are prevalent in Europe and throughout the New World. Although the Indians made cat's cradles too, they thought this to be curious behavior for an adult white man, and a competent interpreter was sent by them to find out exactly what the strange visitor was doing. Lowie immediately hired him. (Parenthetically, we can note that ethnographers have frequently resorted to the role of fool or child as a means of establishing an initial relationship with their informants, not a difficult ruse at all, as this is what the people usually accept them for in the first place.)

Having gained an entree with the Blackfoot, Lowie recorded Wissler's myth, did a bit of ethnography of his own on the side, and then moved on to the Plains Cree. He found the Cree at Hobbema, Alberta, to have lost too much of their native culture to be feasible for study, and, since he was surveying the group only for possible future research, he moved on to his principal ethnographic goal for the season, the Stony Assiniboine. Lowie stayed among the Assiniboine for seven weeks, a short enough field trip by any standards. But it should be duly noted that only two years after this brief sojourn there appeared a monograph of some 270 pages entitled *The Assiniboine* (1909b). Lowie was obviously an indefatigable collector of data. The monograph does not, however, meet the standards of a modern descriptive study. Based almost completely on interviews which dredged out a variety of information on any and all aspects of primitive life, it then reported data without too much attempt to find coherence between them. But the most

The Ethnographer

important result of the 1907 tour came when Wissler sent Lowie orders to proceed to Billings, Montana, and on to the Crow Agency.

Lowie was smitten instantly by the Crow, but he was not able to return to them until 1910. In 1908, the year after his Assiniboine tour, he departed for the first time from his circumnavigation of the Blackfoot to undertake research among the Chipewyans of Lake Athabaska, in northern Alberta and Saskatchewan. This was also to prove to be his only field work outside of the Plains, Southwest and Inter-Montane areas, and his single venture among a Woodlands group.

Lowie's means of transportation were provided by the Hudson's Bay Company, and were just as primitive as the Company's facilities during the halcyon period of the fur trade in the 1820s and 1830s. His voyage took him 105 miles north by stage coach from Edmonton to the Athabaska River, where he was to join a Hudson's Bay supply convoy to the northern trading posts. Arriving at Athabaska Landing, now the modern town of Athabasca, he barely managed to catch the second group of a total expedition of fifteen open, oared scows that were departing for Fort McMurray, 252 miles further north. The scows carried the first provisions for the entire north country since the freeze had set in the previous fall, and the mid-May air was still cool, the river banks still lined with ice left from the recent breakup. The scows were either carried downstream by the current or, occasionally, rowed by the voyageurs, who seemed to spend most of their time singing or playing the Indian-derived hand game. The crew, like the craft, were reminiscent of earlier Hudson's Bay expeditions, for they consisted of a variegated mixture of Orkney Islanders, French Canadians, and Indians. Lowie whiled away part of his time making anthropometric measurements on them, although he knew that the data were genetically worthless, however prized as facts at the time. Lowie found the Chipewyans to be throughly resistant to having their crania and bodies measured, and one can suspect that his attempts hampered his ethnographic efforts. The Indians thought that a person was measured either for a coffin or for the Army, neither of which, understandably, appealed to them, although underlying their manifest objections was the abiding fact that there are few acts more depersonalizing than anthropometry.

Lowie transferred from the open scows to the relative luxury of a wood-burning steamer at Fort McMurray, and reached Fort Chipewyan on Lake Athabaska a few days later. There he was to discover that the situation of the local Canadian Indians was quite different from that of the Indians of the United States. The Hudson's Bay Company had penetrated the area in the late eighteenth century, decades before the fur trade had reached the western United States, and the Indians had seemingly absorbed more of the externals of civilization. Most were nominal Catholics, and all possessed manufactured clothes and other manufactured items. But the aspects of Western culture that had penetrated the north woods were distinctly simple themselves, making the transition less difficult. The Indians still made conical tents and traveled by snowshoe in winter and canoe in the summer; but so did many of the local whites. More important, the Chipewyans had not been confined to reservations, and they maintained a partial autonomy within the system of trading instituted by the Company over a century before Lowie's visit. Social change had taken place among them, to be sure, but the most radical shifts had occurred in the past, and the way of life that Lowie witnessed had been stable for quite a long time.

The Chipewyans, in common with other natives of the north country, had traditionally depended for subsistence on fish, game, and the wild berries and roots of the summer season. They formed very loosely organized bands that usually congregated only for limited periods during the summer. When the fur traders penetrated the country, the Indians soon commenced quite intensive trapping of the small fur-bearing animals that formerly constituted but a minor part of their diet. This new activity shifted the economic center of gravity. Whereas they had once cooperated in the hunting of such large, far-ranging animals as elk, moose, and deer, they now began to pursue the small, nonmigratory, nongregarious, and scattered beaver, marten, and other animals. This activity was easily carried out by families, which staked out claims to small trap-line areas where they spent most of their time and from which they derived much of their livelihood. The larger animals were killed for food when encountered, but the fur bearers yielded the cash needed to buy guns, ammunition, clothing, and ultimately even food supplements. The native political organization became even looser, and the focus of the summer reunions shifted to the trading posts. The Chipewyans depended upon the outside world, but they related to it economically as independent entrepreneurs, not as wage laborers. Moreover, their scattered settlement pattern gave them a degree of isolation from the immediate government surveillance and control that prevailed among their brothers to the south.

Lowie arrived at Fort Chipewyan on June 8, 1908, after more than a month of travel; his visit fortunately coincided with the annual gathering of the Indians to trade furs and to receive annuities from the government. This gathering did not last long, however, for the Indians soon scattered out to their hunting and trapping grounds for the summer season. The total yield of the long and arduous trip was a collection of folk tales and random ethnographic notes. Lowie's trip preceded a later controversy over whether the family trapping territories were post-White products of social change or whether they were bona fide examples of aboriginal private property in land. In 1920 Lowie was to champion the latter view in his book *Primitive Society* (1920:211–12), and thereby add one more arrow to his attack against Lewis Henry Morgan in general and Morgan's notion of primitive communism in particular. But he depended upon Frank Speck's Algonkian research and not upon his own Athapascan experience. Since that time, new evidence seems conclusive that both Speck and Lowie were wrong and that the family hunting grounds were postcontact fur-trapping areas only. Lowie might well have discovered this himself had he followed the Indians out to their trap lines and done research on the economics of native life in the north, but this was neither Lowie's style of research nor was it the kind of investigation that would obviously benefit salvage ethnography. Lowie was never particularly interested in aboriginal economy, and he saw no special purpose in living with the people. When the Indians left Fort Chipewyan, his supply of informants dried up, and he made plans to leave after only a few weeks of unproductive work. This must be admitted to be one of his greatest missed opportunities.

The failure of Lowie's Chipewyan research to shed light upon what was to become a critical question is but one example of the inadequacy of the ethnography of the period. It stemmed in part, as we have noted, from the naturalistic inductivism of the time, which assumed the world, even the social world, to be composed of a myriad of hard, discrete, definable, and finite facts. Culture traits, as transmitted in the units of the memory, fitted in well with this faulty taxonomy and empiricism, which was in congruence with the assumption that most people conformed, or used to conform, to these traditional prescriptions for life. All that seemed necessary was to collect the facts from old informants and you knew what life was like in the past.

But the other element of Lowie's ethnography was the personal one of timidity, reserve, and Victorian manners. His account of the trip to Lake Athabaska casts light on this aspect of the man. He always searched out and prized men of education in the crude society of the frontier. Mr. Kelley, the head of the group of scows that made the trip to Fort McMurray, turned out to have some interesting political views and a good knowledge of Ruskin and Carlyle. He loaned books to Lowie and defended British Imperialism and Disraeli. Lowie summed up Mr. Kelley in a typical phrase, amazing for having been written so late as the 1950s: "Withal he impressed me favorably" (1959:28). He was similarly impressed by the agent at Fort Chipewyan, a Mr. Harris, who had a good library that included Darwin. Lowie traveled with Harris to the latter's home, where he stayed overnight in a room adjoining that of the agent and his wife. He wrote of the night: "Harris was a vigorous man in the prime of life and had been away from home for several weeks. Before long the rhythmic swaying of the conjugal bed conveyed an unequivocal message to the guest nearby" (Lowie 1959: 34). That he should bother to recall this, let alone in such terms, some half century later, surely indicates naïve astonishment at the mundane, biological, and earthy things of life; he exemplified the sheltered middle class intellectual of the period. Plumbing individual

The Ethnographer

minds for social products, Lowie was by disposition a student of the disembodied. Despite his great contributions and successes, he was in many ways an unlikely field worker.

If Lowie focused upon culture as the normative life of a people, he nonetheless understood better than most of his contemporaries that there was more to life than this. His early ethnographic experience, no matter how worthwhile, had placed a stamp upon his view of culture that was partially mitigated by his work with the Crow. His apprenticeship with Wissler had encouraged cursory and superficial investigations that had their value in preserving the outlines of dying cultures, but the Crow gave him the opportunity to study a group in depth and over a long time period. Lowie spent all or part of every summer from 1910 to 1916 among the Crow, plus one more season in 1931; and he kept continually in contact with the reservation through correspondence. Until the time of Malinowski's research in Melanesia in 1914–1918, Lowie's Crow field work was one of the most intensive ever undertaken by a professional ethnographer. His total reportage on the Crow covers approximately two-thousand published pages; few ethnographers have had so much to say about a people as Lowie did about the Crow.

One of the problems of short, survey field work is the necessity to work with interpreters, an impediment that is not always overcome even with a year's experience with a language. Lowie certainly understood the desirability of work in the vernacular, and he usually picked up smatterings of the languages of the people among whom he worked, if only for a superficial rapport. But among the Crow Lowie learned their language well enough to attain a moderate degree of understanding and a reasonable facility in ordinary questioning. He did not work exclusively in the Crow variety of Siouan, however, and always used interpreters, who often worked also as assistants, gathering information on their own for Lowie. Despite his abilities in Crow, Lowie continued to depend upon the interpreters as translators of texts and of material of some profundity and complexity. Thus, an interpreter would be necessary if Lowie were gathering data on Crow cosmology, but he could get by on his own if he were asking persons to identify kinsmen of various categories. He relied upon his understanding of Crow for information on aspects of everyday tribal life, although his interest in the native culture made long interviews a more common technique than participation in ordinary discourse. Lowie was also concerned that his data be absolutely accurate, leading him to such precautions as reviewing with informants and interpreters notes or manuscripts of future publications. He knew that there were inaccuracies in the translation process, but he was evidently more worried about the weakness of his own understanding of Crow than that of his interpreters' English.

Although he spoke Crow better than most anthropologists speak native languages—and modern anthropologists are often less than frank about their linguistic abilities—Lowie simply did not believe that he was fluent in Crow. To him, fluency meant the kind of total bilingualism that he enjoyed in German and English, and he confessed to lapses even there. He took particular exception to Margaret Mead's argument (Mead 1939) that one did not need to be a virtuoso in a language in order to participate in the speech community, and he expressed open disbelief in Mead's allegation that one could learn a language adequately in the course of an ordinary field trip. "No language is easy," he wrote in rejoinder to Mead, and "We use interpreters, not because we like to, but because we have no other choice" (Lowie 1940:89). This was certainly true for the bulk of Lowie's Crow ethnography, but much of his understanding of the Crow, his empathy for them, his feel for the categories in which they thought and expressed themselves, came from his ability to communicate with them. Although his intimate knowledge of the Crow was derived from the same kind of formal interview procedure that he had always used, underneath this veneer was a sense of community with the Crow as people. It is this quality that makes his Crow ethnography so much richer than his other work.

The Crow educated Lowie in the variability of culture within a society. Although the point was often contradicted by the flat way in which he presented his ethnography, Lowie disputed the notion that primitive societies were internally homogeneous, that the individual was submerged in society and was a prisoner of custom. Indeed, one of the points he always made about the Crow was that they were highly individualistic in both war and religion, and he stressed this individuality in his reminiscences of Crow he had known. Nonetheless, one gets the feeling from Lowie's work that he had not fully accounted for this variability in his anthropological theory except to argue that the individual was an active factor in the creation of culture. In his view, there was a culture and there were a people. Each was real, and they were interrelated with each other in a direct way. What was lacking in his systematic view was a mediating arena, a meeting ground between individual personalities and the symbolic realm of culture. In modern anthropological usage, we generally understand this meeting ground to be the social system, or a set of concrete social relationships between interacting individuals. This is social life as it is lived, the practical realm in which human beings sharing some common assumptions and meanings that we call culture manage somehow to get along with one another and to fulfill their individual and collective needs. The aboriginal social nexus is what was lacking among the Crow, whom Lowie knew so well. There was indeed a Crow culture still preserved in the minds of the older people, and there were individuals living on the reservation. But the traditional culture did not find expression in the day-by-day social relations of reservation life. Again, it was the American Indian that impelled Lowie, and most of his contemporaries, to study abstract sets of norms and meanings, apart from concrete social activity. After all, the groups had become memories and had thereby merged with the ideal. Nonetheless, Lowie's work on territoriality and the importance of residence rules was far ahead of the views of his contemporaries, and represents a major step toward an incorporation of social action into cultural theory.

Lowie knew that theory and practice in social life sometimes clashed, although the nature of his information gave him only a limited chance to actually observe the contradictions. He saw a conflict between the Crow ideals of bravery and fearlessness in the face of death, on the one hand, and the valuation of long life on the other. The latter, quite normal, human sentiment caused many warriors to shrink from open acclamation, not so much out of modesty as out of fear that public expectation of their intrepidity would surely result in their deaths.

Lowie's experience among the Hopi in 1915 and 1916 provided him with further evidence that the dominant values of a society were not always realized in action. Here he had one of his few opportunities to study a culture whose social system was still relevant to it and in which he could observe the relation between conduct and ideal. Like other students of the Puebloans, he noted the prevailing ethic of harmony, solidarity, peace, and cooperation. But, unlike many of his contemporaries and successors, he also saw this as an attractive facade for a rather different reality. Beneath the over-all pattern, Lowie found Hopi society to be riven by factionalism and not possessed of any strong sense of tribal unity. The three Hopi villages were separated by mutual hostility, and each community was in turn split into quite discrete households, despite the broader ties of kinship that should have linked them. Gossip was rampant in the Hopi villages, as other ethnographers were to confirm decades later; and below the surface of social life ran a current of fear and suspicion of witchcraft. Ruth Benedict found her Apollonian ideal among the Zuni, and thought it to be a Puebloan characteristic, but Lowie found the Hopi frankly distasteful. He took care to add to his autobiographical memories of the Hopi the warning that this was only a "subjective reaction, not a scientific judgement" (1959:73) but his point was well-taken. That he would not include his evaluation in an ethnographic report, despite its accuracy, is but one more instance of the ideal of "objectivity" toward which he always strove. Lowie would not make statements that might be taken as value judgments on a people he had studied. This same absolute neutrality was to draw criticism some years later in his *Toward Understanding Germany* (1954), which came under attack for not having rendered a judgment on the German people.

Lowie's Crow research was more than an ethnography of a people, for it served as a central vantage point for his view of Plains Indian society. It was during the period encompassing his Crow research that he did his pioneering comparative work on Plains Indian military and age-grade societies, the Sun Dance, and kinship. By 1916, at the age of only thirty-four, he had become internationally known both as an anthropologist and in the larger intellectual community. He was elected President of the American Folklore Society in that year, and in 1917 was invited to Berkeley by Kroeber as Visiting Associate Professor of Anthropology. This was the first step in an association which was to develop into a long academic affiliation. But the Crow years brought him to scholarly maturity, just as it was the Crow experience that was the underpinning of all his later theoretical writing.

World War I must have been a trying period for Lowie, although he does not mention it in his autobiographical writings. Lowie's background in that curious mix of the German literary, scientific, and philosophical traditions, coupled with a Viennese-Jewish childhood and later maturation among the German-American middle-class intelligentsia of New York, produced an ambivalent identity that made the anti-Kaiser rhetoric of the period painful to him. The moral issues were not so clear-cut in 1914 as they were in 1939, and very substantial segments of American society were either neutral regarding the war or leaned toward the Germans. He clearly sympathized with the public position of his old teacher Franz Boas against United States involvement in the war, and defended Boas years later against the charge that he was a German nationalist. What he said of Boas could have been applied as well to himself: "He was an internationalist if ever there was one; but he was also steeped in the culture of his native land, had close relatives living there, was linked by personal and professional ties with innumerable Germans" (Lowie 1947, reprinted in Du Bois 1960:429). But Lowie shrank from the kind of involvement in public causes that characterized Boas. He believed science to be international, objective and dispassionate, and that scientists must rise above the conflicts of their times. In 1914 he published an article in *The New Review* entitled "A Pro-German View," which proclaimed the war to be a simple conflict between German and Russian militarism. Lowie announced that, if one had to choose between the two, he would take the German variety because it at least brought progress with it. He noted, however, that "when internationalism and anti-militarism shall fight to overthrow German nationalism and militarism, I shall be on the side of internationalism" (Lowie 1914a:644). As political analysis, the article was abominable, and Lowie refrained from further comment after American entry into the war. One can also surmise that, always being correct and proper, he saw his duties as an American to be undivided after 1917. Lowie was actually drafted in 1918, but his call-up came on November 11, and he never served.

As Lowie's activity as a field ethnographer slowed down, he became more involved in academic and professional concerns. He served as President of the American Ethnological Society in 1920, and in the same year was appointed to a one-year term as Lecturer in Primitive Law at Columbia University. Lowie had intended to stay in museum work, and had actually refused offers from both the University of California and the University of Washington. His later decision to enter academia proved to be a wise one, but it was not entirely a matter of free choice; the American Museum of Natural History had decided to reward his massive research effort by dropping him. The reason for the dismissal was simple: the Museum had budgetary difficulties and a staff reduction was ordered. The posts of Lowie and of Herbert Spinden, a noted specialist in Mayan prehistory, were eliminated in the cutback. Clark Wissler fought to retain them, but his efforts were futile. Whatever may have been Lowie's feelings for the trustees of the institution, he remained on good terms with Wissler and his surviving staff and always visited the Museum on his trips to New York.

After completing his year on Morningside Heights he accepted the offer of an associate professorship at the University of California, and moved to Berkeley, where he was promoted to a professorship in 1925. For the next twenty years, Lowie and Kroeber formed the core of the Berkeley Department of Anthropology. They were very dissimilar men, but each was essential to the identity of the department; together, they made it into one of the great international centers of anthropological research and graduate education.

Lowie was never a brilliant or charismatic lecturer, the type who fills lecture halls with rapt undergraduates or inspires graduate students to take their mentor's words to an unappreciative profession. But he was organized, informed, solid, and thorough in his delivery, and his courses were packed with information and noted for their cautious and meticulous analysis. Students may not have been transfigured by Lowie's lectures, but they came away knowing a lot of anthropology. Some even felt that they had learned more than they had wanted, for Lowie's love of facts was communicated to the students in heavy reading assignments and dreary detail. Characteristically, Lowie thought his own store of information to be inadequate and uneven. He once told a group of his students that he had run out of material during his first lecture. If this were indeed true, and we can only assume that it was, then he must have spent the rest of his career in an effort to prevent a recurrence of the embarrassment.

Lowie had a profound influence upon generations of Berkeley graduate students, including Julian Steward, Cora Du Bois, Harold Driver, Theodore McCown, Carl Voegelin, Dmitri Shimkin, Ralph Beals, Robert Heizer, George Foster, Robert Spencer—one could go on and on. Just as it was difficult to evaluate Boas's influence upon Lowie, so also is it difficult to say in just what ways Lowie influenced his students. There was indeed a strong tradition of empirical research at Berkeley that could only have been reinforced by Lowie, and he also did much to encourage the study of kinship and social organization. Although his influence was strong, there were few "Lowieites" among the Berkeley students. He wrote: "To be sure, I have not had any urge toward 'leadership' nor toward the establishment of a 'school' of ethnology, and I have, thank God, no disciples" (Lowie 1959:172).

Cora Du Bois has expressed some skepticism at Lowie's disclaimer, for certain of his students, such as Dmitri Shimkin, have expressed strong indebtedness to his ideas and methods (Du Bois 1971). It is nonetheless true that he did not develop a large and active group of followers; acolytes tend to cluster around systems and ideology, and Lowie offered none. Moreover, he was loathe to impose himself upon his students. He insisted upon work and not conformity.

Robert H. Lowie

Lowie did not encourage true believers, but he did not lack admirers among his students. Those who knew him in the 1920s and early 1930s, the great years of Berkeley bohemianism, recall him as an amiable and convivial bachelor, a devoted participant in the Prohibition-days parties held by the students. His preference for tall blonds was notable, and his performance of Crow war dances was considered the high point of an evening. Lowie was on a last name basis with most of his colleagues, in the European tradition, but many of the Berkeley graduate students of the period called him "Robert," although never "Bob." The department was dominated by the paternalistic and rather authoritarian Kroeber, and Lowie was commonly seen as the kindly uncle. Age and his marriage in 1933 had a restraining and sobering influence upon Lowie, and his formality, always present, became the dominant motif in his style. His basic attitude toward students remained unchanged, but he lost his ease of communication with them.

In our present times, it is fashionable among anthropologists to think of all the past generations of anthropologists as Renaissance men who covered all the four branches of anthropology, as well as a good many of the other disciplines. Lowie was by no means such a person, which was possibly all to the good. After all, one could only be an anthropological Renaissance man in a climate in which there was little knowledge in the first place; perhaps 1900 to 1910 was a period when to know a little bit about a lot of things was a virtue, but by the 1920s this was no longer the situation in anthropology. Lowie remained first, last, and always a student of cultural anthropology, unlike Boas and Kroeber, both of whose interests covered three of the four branches. Lowie was, of course, interested in archeological problems insofar as they cast light on his ethnography, but he never published on the subject, and I have no knowledge of his ever having participated in a dig, unless it was while informally visiting colleagues or students. His physical anthropological research was confined to the bit of anthropometry that he did in the field, and for which he received stipends that helped support his ethnography. Otherwise, he published articles refuting racism (cf. Lowie 1914) and dabbled some in eugenics (Lowie 1921). The closest he came

The Ethnographer

to becoming a "general anthropologist" was in linguistics, although his work was largely confined to his studies in Crow grammar (Lowie 1930, 1942). His failure to pursue the subject of linguistics was regretted by him because of the immediacy of its connection with ethnology, but he seemed to have had no qualms or misgivings about his shortcomings in archeology and physical anthropology.

Lowie's less technical books also illustrate his primary identity as an ethnologist. His textbook was entitled *An Introduction to Cultural Anthropology* (Lowie 1934), and that is exactly what it was. The 1917 forerunner of this work, *Culture and Ethnology* (Lowie 1917a), was equally committed to ethnology as a science in itself; and his two other best-known works, *Primitive Society* (1920) and *Primitive Religion* (1924), were equally circumscribed. And when Lowie chose to write a history of his discipline, the title chosen was *The History of Ethnological Theory* (1937). Although Lowie was far from being parochial, and actually read widely in the other branches of anthropology, he had a fine sense of his own limitations and a true respect for the complexity and integrity of the field of ethnology. Since his time, the discipline has grown enormously, and, with this growth, we have witnessed an increasing specialization and separation of the branches of the profession. Lowie was not narrow, just ahead of his times. But he brought this sense of specialization to his students, and, in a department that was otherwise committed to everybody's doing everything, he gave a sense of focus and discipline. I vividly remember my own sense of puzzlement at the variegated activities of some graduate students at Berkeley when I went there in 1955. They seemed to be hopping from research in ethnology to archeological trips to sessions with linguistic informants—and getting nowhere with any of their efforts. Lowie, and the students he still had after his retirement in 1951, seemed by contrast to be pillars of steadfast and serious professional endeavor.

The two great changes in Lowie's middle years were his shift from museum work and intensive field research to the academic life, and his marriage to Luella Cole in 1933. Lowie was fifty years old when he married for the first and only time, and this too seems to fit the

Robert H. Lowie

man. I have no information on whether he had come at all close to marital status in the past, but so important a step would certainly have merited Lowie's most careful consideration. He was a Romantic in the tradition of Goethe rather than of Byron, and he was certainly not given to impetuousness. It should also be noted that he did not marry until after his mother's death. Although a late marriage, it was the kind of close relationship that one often finds among childless couples; and to one who did not know Lowie for long, it was hard to imagine him as having been a bachelor for most of his adult life. The Lowies complemented each other well. She was a psychologist and conversant with his interests; he, in turn, maintained an active concern with her field. Robert Lowie was steeped in the European tradition; Luella Cole Lowie, on the other hand, came from an old American family. He was shy and formal in style; she was direct, bluff, and frank. After Lowie's death in 1957, his widow became his literary executor, and it was through her efforts that a substantial amount of Lowie's unpublished work has been brought to print. She died in 1970 in Berkeley.

Lowie continued to publish on his Plains research after joining the Berkeley faculty, but did little field work. He wrote prolifically, as the above references to some of his books show, and his interests ranged throughout cultural anthropology, although with special emphasis on kinship and religion. His books gave Lowie a much wider audience than the handful of anthropologists of his time, and their generality established him as a leading social theorist. The most important of the seven general works that he published in his middle years, between 1917 and 1937, was *Primitive Society*, a book which he later confessed to having written too quickly because of a tight publisher's deadline. We will give detailed attention to this work in a subsequent section, but it should be noted now that it established Lowie as one of the leaders of the attack against cultural evolutionism. It is still widely read, and its merits vigorously debated. The fact that anthropologists still argue over it a half century after its first publication is but one token of its seminal importance. Although Lowie was given to modesty about his contribution to theory, his late American Museum and early Berkeley years were most productive.

Curiously, Lowie's most important ethnographic involvement while at Berkeley did not actually bring him to the field and took him far away from his North American specialty. In 1924 Lowie returned to Europe for the first time since he had left as a ten-year-old boy. He had become editor of the *American Anthropologist* in that year and was attending the International Congress of Americanists in Sweden as a young scholar of growing importance. While in Europe he met many of the great European anthropologists, most prominently Father Wilhelm Schmidt, Baron Erland Nordenskiöld, and Dr. Paul Rivet. These men were not only pre-eminent in their profession, but were also, especially Rivet and Nordenskiöld, very interested in South America. As an Americanist, it was understandable that Lowie should find the South American Indians a logical extension of his previous work, but he must have become additionally absorbed through the problems in social organization posed by the area. Nordenskiöld and Rivet were most eager to pull together the fragmentary and scattered information on the South American continent, and Lowie found their suggestion for a handbook of South American Indians to be an attractive one. In the following year, Nordenskiöld wrote to Lowie to tell him of an interesting fellow named "Nimuendajú" who lived in Belém do Pará, Brazil, and who was deeply engaged in ethnography. Lowie noted this, filing the information away in his mind.

Some ten years later, Karl Izikowitz, a noted South Americanist and a student of Nordenskiöld, wrote to Lowie of Nimuendajú's need for funds, and Lowie undertook to help him, starting a decade of collaboration by mail. Lowie provided professional experience, manuscript translation, and some funds, while Nimuendajú did field work. Strangely, the two men never met. Nimuendajú was one of the most fascinating ethnographers of the century. Born Kurt Unkel in Germany, he studied for a year at Uppsala and then moved to Brazil, where he did extensive field work among the Gê-speaking groups of Maranhão, Goias, and Pará, states. The Indians dubbed him

Robert H. Lowie

Nimuendajú, and he kept the name. It was appropriate, for he was married to an Indian woman and lived much as did his informants while in the field. Out of the Lowie-Nimuendajú collaboration came monographs on the Apinayé, the Eastern Timbira, the Serente, and the Tukuna. The first three volumes were translated from the German by Lowie, but the last, written in Portuguese, was translated by William Hohenthal, one of Lowie's students.

The Nimuendajú collaboration also resulted in Lowie's complete immersion in the South American literature, an interest which proved most useful as plans for a massive summary of the area developed. In 1931 Lowie became Chairman of the Division of Anthropology and Psychology of the National Research Council, and in the following year revived the Rivet-Nordenskiöld proposal for a handbook on South American Indians. The Division approved the project but did little about it, finally turning the matter over to the Smithsonian Institution. There, it was revived again and ultimately grew into a six-volume work under the leadership of Julian Steward (Steward 1946–1950). Lowie continued to maintain an active interest in the "Handbook of South American Indians" and contributed several of the ethnographic sections, as well as comparative summaries of social and political organization and property among the Marginal and Tropical Forest tribes of the jungle and savannah lowlands. Lowie regarded his efforts retrospectively as having been a diversion from his true interests in the Plains Indians, but subsequent students of South American Indians found that the Nimuendajú work and the "Handbook" opened up the continent to them. Such distractions from his main concerns were quite common with Lowie, and he often allowed the interests of the moment to carry him along. This was not out of character, however, for Lowie was not at all a rigid man. Outwardly he seemed so, for he fairly exuded discipline and form. The real man, as suggested before, was much softer and more pliant, and the South American venture was but one more example of his willingness to set aside the primary interests and concerns of his career. Nonetheless, by staying within the confines of cultural anthropology, he maintained a clearer direction than did most of his contemporaries.

The Ethnographer

His South American period had its scholarly rationale as a continuation of the studies of an Americanist, but it had other roots too. Among the most important was the fact that Nimuendajú was a German, and this added greatly to the sympathy that Lowie felt for this lone and impoverished scholar doing important work under such difficult circumstances. Lowie's deep attachment to German culture and the German people came under severe trial during the 1930s with the rise of the Third Reich. He was unequivocally opposed to Nazism, for it was contrary to all the rationalist and internationalist ideals that underlay his science. His Germans were the literati, not the technocrats and soldiers; the great German period, for Lowie, was not that of Kaiser Wilhelm, or even Bismarck, but that of the Revolution of 1848. There was also the fact of his part-Jewish ancestry, which he did not try to hide or deliberately suppress; rather, he treated the matter as irrelevant and inconsistent with his identity as a product of the Germanic scientific and humanistic tradition. Indeed, the closest that he comes to mentioning his Jewish descent in print is in defense of his book *Toward Understanding Germany*, which many reviewers felt was insufficiently condemnatory. Lowie wrote:

✢ *Some have even gone so far as to accuse me of having written an apology for the Germans; this notion is absurd, if for no other reason than that the Nazi regime liquidated almost all my European relatives. Although I was not especially close to them, I was certainly not amiably disposed toward a government that sent them to be destroyed in Polish furnaces (Lowie 1959:144).*

Nonetheless, Lowie never published his anti-Nazi views during the period up to 1945, although he had printed his "pro-German view" in 1914. Despite this early and naïve fling at political writing, all of his later work exemplified the credo that he set out, appropriately, in his contribution to the *festschrift* for his old friend Paul Radin:

✢ *The test of the mature ethnologist is the extent to which he can extend the axioms of his professional creed to cover cases in* which he is emotionally involved. The pitfalls are innumerable, and hardly anyone will succeed in avoiding all of them. But the ethnologist worthy of his salt will make a determined effort to rise above the partisan level, to project himself into the minds of others—even if they are his fellow-citizens—and to view his own culture from within (Lowie 1960:159).

Despite his passion for "objectivity," it was inevitable that Lowie should be drawn by the German disaster into an analysis of its roots. He embarked upon this voyage of self-discovery by participation in a training course for the Army at Berkeley in 1943. His undivided commitment is bespoken by the fact that he was lecturing on Germany and the Balkans to American troops who were to invade and occupy the region. Academically, his lectures eventuated in a short book entitled *The German People: A Social Portrait to 1914* (Lowie 1945). Upon his retirement in 1950, Lowie was encouraged by Paul Fejos of the Wenner-Gren Foundation in New York to undertake actual field work in Germany, and he and his wife spent from September 1950 to March 1951 touring the country, talking to people from all walks of life, not only academics, reading, and generally gathering impressions.

Lowie's German experience was a departure from his life's work. He had embarked upon the study of an urban industrial society, although he had previously never paid much attention to anything even as complex as a peasantry. Moreover, it was a society with which he was closely identified. He was also working completely, and for the first time, in the native language. The shift in style of ethnographic technique is interesting. The Lowies gave rides to hitchhikers and engaged them in long and open-ended conversation. They watched people in restaurants and railway stations, they chatted with students, they overheard snippets of conversations, and in all learned about Germany from their own interaction with the people. Lowie observed: "These small and seemingly insignificant bits sometimes tell more about a culture than a formal interview does" (Lowie 1959:154).

Lowie enjoyed native linguistic facility in German, but, for all

The Ethnographer

his Continental manners, it should be remembered that he had spent almost all his long life in the United States; Germany was really foreign to him. The behavior, both everyday and formal, of the Germans was fascinating to him, and he also developed a deep interest in the categories in which the people spoke and, perhaps, thought. Sensitive to the nuances of speech and behavior that are overlooked by the true native, he was sufficiently fluent in German to catch them. The profuse use of titles by the Germans intrigued him, and he was taken by the fine lines that determined whether a person should be addressed by the informal and diminutive "du" or by the formal and respectful "sie."

Characteristically, the result of Lowie's research was not a neat, encapsulated, and oversimplified view but a mosaic. He rejected completely the national character approach that was then in vogue and best exemplified by Ruth Benedict's *The Chrysanthemum and the Sword* (1946), which attempted to limn the characterology of the Japanese people, the imbedment of Japanese culture in the personality of the "typical" or "average" Japanese. Lowie believed that this method assumed a generality and stability of both culture and personality that was empirically untrue and, therefore, at best misleading. His own analysis of Germany took ample account of the subvarieties of German culture, and of the fact that German culture was not distinctive but merged at the political frontiers with other varieties of Western European culture. He also showed that the patterns were not stable over time, arguing that it was perfectly plausible that Germany could develop political democracy and was not doomed to authoritarianism by a deep character flaw. As for Nazism, he said that many Germans adopted it only out of expediency, while many others actively opposed the movement. The Germans, he said, did not plunge into the horror with eyes open and the future clear. Rather, they drifted with history into a catastrophe whose unfolding they did not comprehend. This was indeed, a kindly view to take of Germany in 1950, and many Americans did not understand it. But we have since that time witnessed the process that drew America along a path that led from the sending of a few military advisers to a little Southeast Asian country to its end at Mylai. There is a parable here, but there is still no way out of Lowie's dilemma or that of the German scholars—or that of Americans. To understand history in retrospect does not mean that we should be passive to its happening. The silence and withdrawal of the scholar, his "objectivity," are not the virtues that Lowie thought them to be.

Lowie's later years brought him almost every honor that the profession had to bestow. He was the Thomas H. Huxley Memorial Medalist and Lecturer in England in 1948, and received the Viking Medal later in the same year. His German research was interrupted many times for lectures and the bestowal of honorary memberships in scientific societies. During his retirement, he taught at Columbia, Harvard, the University of Washington, and the University of Hamburg, as well as lecturing at campuses throughout the country. He also conducted his annual seminar at Berkeley until his death. The University of California bestowed a final honor upon him posthumously when, in 1960, the Robert H. Lowie Museum of Anthropology was dedicated on the Berkeley campus.

Lowie's last seminar at Berkeley was given in the spring semester of 1957. The subject was, appropriately, the Plains Indians. He appeared drawn and tired as the semester opened, and after a short time he was unable to attend. I kept the seminar going at Lowie's request, although I am afraid that its only highlight was the day when David Mandelbaum and E. Adamson Hoebel joined us, to add the Plains Cree and the Comanche, respectively, to my Eastern Shoshone material. Somehow, we always came back to the Crow. Toward the end of the school year, Lowie's condition improved somewhat, and he invited the seminar to meet in his house. His cancer was clearly advanced, but he listened intently to the students, commented on their papers, and brought the course to the end of the semester. There was an unmistakable sense of closure and finality to it. On September 21 he read his wife a section from *Faust*, fell into sleep, and died.

Perhaps the key to Lowie's greatness as an ethnologist was the marginal status that he ascribed to himself. A German in America,

The Social Theorist

he proved also to be an American in Germany. He never exactly fitted in anywhere, for the Germany of his mind was that of his father and grandfather, whereas the America of his life was the middle class German community of the upper East Side of New York and the Indian reservations of the western United States. Wherever he was, he was able to stand off from an ambience that did not envelope and include him. He was *degagé* and estranged, surrounded by a shell of formality which protected him from a world in which he did not really belong. His total decorum also served to shield a very vulnerable and sensitive person who committed himself so totally to friendships that only the appearance of aloofness allowed him to survive human relationships. It is this quality that all who knew him remember fondly. But beyond the fact that he was indeed a lovely man, this simultaneous capacity for cultural removal and personal closeness is a testimonial to his total identity as an ethnologist.

LOWIE THE SOCIAL THEORIST

Contemporary students of anthropology have a regrettable penchant for looking upon the early part of the twentieth century in their discipline as a period of intellectual aridity and sterility. The late nineteenth century appears as a period of giants, one in which men like Lewis Henry Morgan, Edward B. Tylor, J. F. McLennan, and Henry Maine created vast syntheses of human culture that overcame in grandeur and boldness whatever empirical deficiencies they may have suffered. The beginning of our own century, in contrast, saw the destruction of these theoretical edifices and the beginning of a tradition noted for its caution, its obsession with fact, and its unwillingness to venture into speculation. As with many of our images of the past, there is much nonsense in this view. For those such as Boas and his students, who forged a discipline out of a curiosity, this was a time of unusual excitement and innovation. It was a period in which a plethora of contrasting views contended with one another and in which all of the methodological and epistemological canons of the past were being challenged. Today's students should, therefore, find it of consummate interest, for much the same turmoil is occurring in the social sciences today. But, whereas anthropology as a discipline is now only undergoing transformation, in Lowie's time it was being born.

When Lowie entered anthropology, the most pervasive view of man was that of the evolutionists. The term "evolution" has been used in many ways by anthropologists and biologists. It may be taken to indicate merely that change is orderly and, when seen in retrospect, directional. Others view evolution as a progressive process in which organisms, whether biological or cultural, move on to increasingly complex and broad forms of organization. Evolution may also be used in the simple, biological sense of organic change and differentiation, of specialized adaptation to an environment. Or, finally, one may interpret evolution to mean the over-all panorama of the unfolding and emergence of forms of life, be they organic or social. It was the latter sense of evolution as the total history of man and his cultures which was the dominant view of early anthropology.

Evolutionism fitted the mood of the nineteenth century. It was nourished by the Enlightenment belief in man's perfectability, and faith in the steady movement of society toward the realization of both freedom and rationality. Western man, in Europe and North America, was looked upon as the apical achievement of the human species and as the base line from which further progress would be made. Man was his own maker, the product of his own intelligence, the mold of his destiny. The growth of biological theories of evolution during the nineteenth century may perhaps have cast a shadow over this belief that man was *sui generis* and the creation of his own mind, but biology also did much to reinforce the accompanying belief in the irreversibility and regularity of progress.

Charles Darwin's *Origin of Species* appeared in 1859, and his *The Descent of Man* was published in 1871, but neither work could be said to have preceded or caused the florescence of evolutionary theory as applied to culture. The only prominent cultural evolutionist to specifically adopt Darwin's view of natural selection as a principal mechanism of evolution was Herbert Spencer, whose earlier publications on human progress had preceded Darwin's work.

The Social Theorist

Other early cultural evolutionists included J. F. McLennan, who published his classic *Primitive Marriage* in 1865, and Sir Edward Burnett Tylor, whose *Researches into the Early History of Mankind and the Development of Civilization* appeared in the same year. The great American champion of cultural evolutionism, Lewis Henry Morgan, was not a Darwinian in any sense of the word, and his work, too, is so close in time to that of Darwin that one need not think that influence was inevitable. Morgan's study of kinship, *Systems of Consanguinity and Affinity of the Human Family* appeared in 1870, a year before *The Descent of Man;* and *Ancient Society,* his overview of cultural evolution, was published in 1877. Darwin, then, was part of a trend that found its theme in progress and its method in taxonomy, or classification, although it must be recognized that, among his contemporaries, he was the greatest and most notable contributor.

Darwin's success was because he outlined the *processes* of evolution, something which his counterparts in the study of cultural evolution largely neglected. Morgan, especially, dedicated himself to the study of the entire tableau of human history and to the delineation of what he believed were the stages of society through which man progressed, and through which he *had to* progress, on his path to civilization. That Morgan had little of enduring importance to say on *how* it happened is indicated by the fact that anthropologists still have lively arguments over whether Morgan was a materialist or an idealist. Morgan's scheme outlined three principal phases of cultural evolution. In order of their emergence, these were Savagery, Barbarism, and Civilization; the first two were further subdivided into lower, middle, and upper periods. Each of these stages and substages was associated with a characteristic technological feature, although he did not attribute the phase to the technology, and each also exemplified certain social institutions. In Lower Savagery, promiscuity was the first form of mating, followed by group marriage of brothers and sisters, real and collateral, or Morgan's "consanguine family." Morgan found this to be still reflected in what he called "Malayan" kinship terminology—what we call today the "Hawaiian" system—which distinguishes relatives only by their generation and sex, lumping together all kin of each sex on one's own generation. Man, according to Morgan's scheme, developed in Middle Savagery a form of group marriage in which unions between brothers and sisters were prohibited but in which classes of men and women married as units. According to the logic of this marriage system, any man of the group could be the father of a child, and mothers were not well distinguished by function; therefore, the men were all called father and the women mother, and all children of the group were brothers and sisters. This formed the basis of Morgan's "Turanian-Ganowanian" kin term systems, or what we now call Iroquois kinship (see Fig. 1, p. 63 below). In such systems, the father's brothers are identified by the father term, the mother's sisters by the mother term, and their children are called brother and sister. The father's sisters, the mother's brothers, and their children are called by separate terms, which we usually translate as aunt, uncle, and cousin, respectively.

The essential underpinnings of evolutionism rested on a belief that living primitives represented stages of man's history and that we could find vestiges of the past in their societies or in certain primitive institutions and customs. Morgan had no examples of promiscuity and incestuous union to offer, simply because these are not standard or approved mating forms in any society, although they, of course, occur sporadically as deviations. Rather, his evidence consisted of kinship terms, usages which he believed to be relatively unchanging and not even transferable by borrowing. The terms were thus believed to be survivals, or unchanging residues, of a postulated past. Where Morgan found very similar usages in different societies, he believed that the two groups must have once been united in a very remote past and had subsequently become separated by migration. It was all highly speculative. When he got to his higher evolutionary levels, especially to Upper Savagery and the various phases of Barbarism, he was on firmer ground. He thought that paired marriages, including polygamy, arose from group marriage and that the marriage sets associated with group marriage gave way to the matrilineal clan. The matri-clan, a group of people finding common descent in the female line from some remote ancestor and governed by the exogamic rule that one must marry out of his clan, seemed to him the logical original form of descent, as people were still unaware of the facts of paternity and could, therefore, only reckon ties through women. Morgan conceived of the clan as a total social form, an entire polity based on criteria of sex and blood relationship but encompassing the total social life of a group. The clan lasted from Upper Savagery through most of Barbarism, yielding finally to patriarchal rule under the pressure of growing property relationships and the recognition of biological paternity.

The latter shift to patriliny and patriarchy was one of the few clear instances of material causality in Morgan's evolutionism, for the transitions to other stages were generally attributed by him to the unfolding of a natural progression of ideas. But the scheme attracted the attention of Marx and Engels, forming the basis for Engels's *The Origin of the Family, Private Property, and the State* 1884; Eng. tr., 1902). Engels's book was far superior to Morgan's *Ancient Society*, which would probably be a little-known curio today if it had not fallen under the interpretation of better minds than Morgan's. In Lowie's time, however, *Ancient Society* was still a basic source, and Lowie undertook to attack it, along with all the rest of evolutionism.

It is difficult to separate from the total corpus of Lowie's writings those that are specifically antievolutionary, for his entire approach was antithetical to that tradition, his works shot through with criticisms of it. Lowie, like his mentor Boas, insisted upon canons of proof that approximated those of the physical sciences, an attitude which induced a profound skepticism about any theory that pretended to reconstruct the early history of man by reference to a few tables of kinship terms and a Victorian view of marriage. As a student of Mach, he believed fervently in science, and he hoped almost as fervently for the development of scientifically arrived at laws of culture. He thought, however, that the only proper scientific mood was one of caution and absolute empiricism. Thus, operating on the assumption that unilinear evolutionism rested on the phenomenon of independent and parallel reinvention of culture traits, he attempted to show that innovations come about most commonly through intercultural borrowing.

The most tenable hypotheses to Lowie were those that made the fewest axiomatic assumptions and thus could be stated most economically. When faced with the choice of deciding whether an item of culture was indigenous to a society and independently invented by it or whether it had come to it through borrowing from another society, he always opted for the latter, all other things being equal. He knew that, although many elements of culture were independently reinvented in different societies, most traits in any culture were received through diffusion. Simple statistical probability would therefore impel him to accept the diffusionary explanation unless specific evidence to the contrary were available. Moreover, independent inventions always assume a series of processes for which evidence was often absent, and Lowie did not operate on the basis of unproven premises. Diffusion was a more economical supposition to him, and thus preferable. Lowie was not so much given to historicism as to the dictum of "Occam's Razor": "multiplicity ought not to be posited without necessity." Stated baldly, the simplest explanation is the best explanation. To be sure, however, it can sometimes be wrong.

Lowie's bent for the diffusionist explanation is neatly illustrated in his article "Some Problems of Geographical Distribution" (1951), in which he took a series of myths found in western North America and Tierra del Fuego showing certain key similarities and attributed the parallels to the migration of peoples in an archaic age down through the Great Basin and ultimately to southernmost South America. The migrants presumably left behind traces of their myths, traces which are not found in the intervening areas of their migration route, supposedly because of the development of more complex societies and cultures there. The stories, which deal with the origin of work, are thus an archaic residue to be found in the simplest societies of the New World and explainable by the movement of peoples and diffusion. The question arises whether this is indeed the simplest explanation. Which would be more remarkable: that peoples some 6,000 miles apart should independently invent the same theme, or that once contiguous groups should maintain substantially similar stories for over ten millennia after their separation?

Actually, I recorded a story among the Amazonian Mundurucú which told of a time when axes and hoes worked by themselves, but through the disobedience of man a culture hero decreed that men would have to wield them thenceforward through their own labor (Murphy 1958:80-81). The story is of additional interest, for it was merged with the Biblical book of Genesis, in which the origin of work is, of course, one of the results of man's fall from grace. Is it, then, so unusual for man to speculate on why he must toil that we should postulate a single origin for the tale? Although the Mundurucú story differed from the Lowie examples in that both of the latter involved two brothers, there are several other Mundurucú tales, and indeed ones from all over the New World, that feature brothers. There is usually a dualism in these themes that is too general to be traceable to diffusion. Even if we will never know for certain whether the North American and Fuegian tales were diffused or are true independent parallels, perhaps the question is not critical. Either explanation would require one to assume an enormous tenacity, an inherent appeal in the theme, and the question of parallelism or diffusion may be adventitious. Both borrowing and invention must ultimately rely upon the fact that the story must have served some function, whether social or psychological, which would at once explain either its creation or its acceptance and perpetuation.

To continue the theme of diffusion vs. independent invention, as it has often been termed, it was the firm belief of Lowie and his contemporaries that the neat stages of the evolutionists were totally negated by the phenomenon of diffusion, or the transfer of culture traits from one society to another. The evolutionists' tenet that there was a unilinear progression to the history of mankind in which certain institutions appeared in clusters at certain periods and were the preconditions for further progress seemed to them to be at best an ideal tendency and at its worst simple nonsense. How could a culture trait be indicative of a unilinear stage of evolution if it became widely disseminated among societies of varying complexity and differing cultures? One of Lowie's favorite examples was that of the bow and arrow, which had been diffused throughout the New World and were used by the simplest of hunters and collectors as well as by the armies of great states. This was enough to place even the rudest of the American Indians in the stage of Upper Savagery, one notch above the Polynesians, whose islands had not been reached by the weapon (cf. Lowie 1937:57). Yet, the Polynesians were consummate navigators and skilled agriculturalists, possessing stratified societies of remarkable sophistication. Obviously, in this case the progress of the Polynesians had little to do with whether or not they used the bow and arrow. In other technological items, entire stages of evolution were simply bypassed. One common assumption of the evolutionists was that man emerged from the Stone Age to the use of copper, thence to bronze, and finally to iron. This sequence is borne out by Near Eastern archeology and undoubtedly represents the actual world-wide sequence of the emergence of the inventions. But, as Lowie pointed out, the Africans went directly from the Stone Age to an Iron Age through borrowing (Lowie 1917a:81).

One might defend the evolutionary position by stating that the histories of particular societies are not in question and that we are actually concerned with the sequence of emergence of institutions and inventions in the over-all history of mankind. This is what Marshall Sahlins and Elman Service have tried to do under the rubric of "general evolution" (Sahlins and Service 1960). Under these circumstances, the bypassing of stages here and there is unimportant, for while particular societies have their ups and downs and vagaries, progress is inevitable and each step has its preconditions in the past. Surely, the wheel came before the automobile and gunpowder before the atom bomb. This is obviously true, and Lowie would have agreed if he had thought it to be an especially illuminating idea (which he would not have); but the evolutionary theories that he battled dealt with the emergence of social institutions and ideas, as well as technology, and most of the evolutionists in question did indeed believe, despite some scholarly hedging, that societies had to go through one stage to get to the next. Morgan thought that the ultimate progress of a society must recapitulate that of mankind, and with some modifications so did many of his contemporaries.

The Social Theorist

Lowie's most effective critique of cultural evolution centered on theories of kinship and the family. We will have occasion later to comment on his very important and constructive contributions to this field. But he tore down as he built. His most important book, *Primitive Society* (1920), was looked upon as overly negative and cautious by Alfred L. Kroeber and W. H. R. Rivers, but it stood as the first general work on primitive social organization since Morgan, and was representative of most of the shifts in theory since that time. In *Primitive Society* Lowie did not address himself to a systematic and logical destruction of evolutionism but instead largely allowed the data to do the job. He believed that Morgan chose promiscuity, with incest, as the earliest form of mating simply because it seemed a logical zero point from which to start (Lowie 1920:56). Most anthropologists today would agree that before there was marriage there was no marriage and, therefore, mating was promiscuous, at least from the point of view of a *moral* order. But they would also agree that such a phase would hardly be a stage of human *culture,* simply because there was no moral order. Lowie went on to argue that Morgan's next stage, in which brother-sister unions were permitted but intergenerational mating tabooed, was based only on kinship terms. Lowie correctly pointed out that Morgan believed that those using "Malayan," or Hawaiian, terminology confused "father" with "procreator" (Lowie 1920:58–59). Social paternity and procreation are not, of course, the same thing, and generations of anthropologists since Lowie's time have agreed with his basic premise that relationship terms group people according to common social characteristics and not by blood ties.

One of the most prevalent of all evolutionary notions states that matrilineality precedes patrilineality in the evolution of descent. There is considerable evidence in support of this view even today, for, although we have several instances of transition from matrilineality to patrilineality, there are few well-documented cases of the reverse process. But Morgan, at least, said much more than this. According to his theory, after marriage classes the next form of kinship organization is the matrilineal clan, and it is only late in the evolution of culture that the family emerges as an independent unit. The clan supposedly appears in savagery and persists through most of the periods of Barbarism, and since all North American Indians were in this phase they should all have formed clans. Lowie notes that John Swanton's research conclusively disproved this notion, for clans were absent in a good deal of western North America (Lowie 1920:150 ff). Indeed, Lowie's first field work, it will be remembered, was among the Shoshone, who had little in the way of a stable sociopolitical organization above the level of the family. Lowie's later work among the Crow brought him into direct contact with matrilineal clans, but he was also aware that any form of unilineal descent was rare on the Plains.

The North American data revealed a pattern quite contrary to that perceived by Morgan. Most of the simpler hunting and collecting societies were clanless and had clearly bilateral family arrangements. On the contrary, clanship was most commonly found among the more advanced groups, such as the agriculturalists of the eastern United States, the Puebloans of the Southwest and the prosperous fishing groups of the British Columbian and Alaskan littorals. Lowie concluded from this, and from the evidence of other continents, that the customary evolutionary sequence must be reversed: unilineal descent groups, whether matrilineal or patrilineal, grow out of an earlier period in which the family was the principal kin group. Underlying the growth of unilineal descent units was the development of laws of inheritance and rules of unilocal residence—according to which a married couple reside permanently with the kin of one spouse as opposed to the other. Lowie wrote:

> *Finally, the multiple origin of the sib, which was previously suggested on other grounds, is rendered still more likely if underlying the sib are phenomena such as the residence rule or inheritance law. For in these rules lay the possibility for an indefinite number of independent developments of patrilineal and matrilineal descent (Lowie 1920:162).*

If the sib, a term under which Lowie subsumed both patrilineal and matrilineal descent groups, indeed emerged from such material conditions as inheritance and residence, and if it did have multiple origins, then the supposed inevitable priority of matrilineality over patrilineality was dubious on the face of it. Lowie also marshaled his data to show that the sib was transferable by diffusion, as in the case of the supposed Gros Ventre adoption of Blackfoot kin patterns, an unfortunately dubious example. He also was among the first to attack the doctrine of survivals, the method of conjectural history by which the evolutionists attempted to show traces of matrilineal institutions within patrilineal societies and thus prove the priority of the female principle. Lowie selected Tylor's use of the special relation between the mother's brother and the sister's son, the so-called avunculate, as an indicator of former matrilineality, showing the custom to be a diffusable one often absent in matrilineal societies and sometimes associated with cross-cousin marriage, thus making the relationship an affinal one. He concluded his attack by a broad survey indicating that patrilineal sibs, or at least patrilineal tendencies in sibless societies, were found in both advanced groups and quite simple ones:

> *It is true that the highest known civilizations, like those of the Chinese, the ancient Greeks, and our own, are predominantly patrilineal. But this also holds for the lowest known cultures so far as either side is stressed at all, while the position of matrilineal peoples is intermediate* (Lowie 1920:182).

It should be kept in mind that when Lowie spoke of "highest" and "lowest" civilizations or cultures he was using *implicit* criteria of over-all social complexity and, more importantly, technology. And when he spoke of residence rules as producing aggregates of co-resident people having a form of relationship conducive to the development of unilineal institutions, he discussed the influence of the division of labor upon residence. This raises the possibility that Lowie was not so complete an antievolutionist as he seemed. The truth is that he was not. Rather, he was totally opposed to what he considered the slapdash, speculative, and fanciful procedures of the unilineal evolutionists, and he was actually more anti-Morgan than antievolutionist. Marvin Harris recognizes this in his *The Rise of Anthropological Theory*, although he characterizes Lowie as an antimaterialist (Harris 1968:343–72). In view of the above-mentioned aspects of Lowie's view of social organization, also discussed by Harris (*ibid.* 350), even this charge is debatable. To be sure, Lowie took issue at many points with doctrinaire economic determinism, but he always followed the evidence as he saw it. Although he disagreed with Morgan's notions on primitive communism in land, citing Speck's erroneous conclusions on Algonkian family hunting territories, he nonetheless recognized that freehold, individual title to natural resources, such as exists in our own society, is rare among primitives. What he did in his discussion of property in *Primitive Society* was ask what exactly was meant by "primitive communism." Who owned what, when, where, how, and with whom? He concluded that one should not make a simplistic division between communism and individuality, for both terms covered many possible arrangements. In the final analysis, he agreed with Sir Henry Maine that corporate ownership by kin groups or other social units, and not communism, was the key institution in primitive societies. This taking apart of broad, loosely phrased concepts was characteristic of Lowie's method, for he had earlier asked what Morgan was talking about when he said "clan" (Lowie 1914c). He proceeded to show that unilineal descent groups were not of a piece but had many differences in both form and function, varying even in their relation to rules of exogamy. Clanship, being diverse and multifunctional, thereby lost its panhuman nature, which, after all, was its only significance in any scheme of unilinear evolution. Perhaps Lowie did take apart more than he put back together, but this, as he said, was part of any rationalist critique:

> ✛ *Every destructive criticism of a view sanctioned by tradition leaves it adherents with a sense of loss. This feeling is of course an illusion, for there is no real loss when opinions are abandoned that are demonstrably false (Lowie 1914c:93–94).*

He would have said the same thing about theology—and none of the anthropologists who have found him to be negative and destructive would have faulted him for it.

The Social Theorist

Lowie, although more than any other of his contemporaries responsible for the eclipse of evolutionary theory in anthropology, was too fair-minded and conscious of the importance of history to dismiss his predecessors. He wrote that Morgan:

> ✤ *expressed no enlightening ideas on art, language or religion; but he can never be ignored by the student of kinship. His was not a flashy intellect, but one of unusual honesty, depth and tenacity; and prolonged groping rewarded his real, if drab, intelligence with glimpses of true insight. There is no better illustration of Darwin's saying, "it's dogged does it"* (Lowie 1937:67).

Admirers of Morgan may interpret this as an *ad hominem* attack. Others, who have plowed through the tedious writing and startlingly naïve thinking of *Ancient Society*, will say that the appraisal is perfectly justified. But Lowie gave Morgan due credit for opening up the entire scientific study of kinship, and he was quick to announce Morgan's accuracy regarding the presence of clans among the Crow (Lowie 1936:170).

A good deal of Lowie's critique depended upon the influence of diffusion, but he took care to note that the evolutionists were completely aware of the process. Morgan, for example, thought that the clan had a single origin and diffused throughout the world because of a biological superiority that he believed derived from exogamy and the denial of brother-sister incest. A good deal of Lowie's "History of the Sib" chapter in *Primitive Society* was devoted to showing that the clan had multiple origins; in this instance he was championing independent invention over the diffusionism of Morgan! And Lowie was well aware of Tylor's study tracing the Aztec game of patolli to the Hindu game of pachisi, as fine an example of diffusionist thought as one can find. Tylor, he wrote, was saved from becoming an extreme diffusionist only because he exercised very strict canons of evidence (Lowie 1937:75–76). The trouble with the evolutionists, according to Lowie, was not that they ignored diffusion but that they did not fit it successfully into their evolutionary schemes. Even if one grants the sequence of

Robert H. Lowie

stages to be true, how is it to be empirically demonstrated if it is being continually disturbed by outside influences (Lowie 1946:230)?

Lowie was an historicist, but he was not an extreme diffusionist of the school he held in the same low regard as that of evolutionism. Rather, he took the quite respectable, although mechanistic, position that the cause of any cultural phenomenon must be sought in its cultural antecedents. To Lowie culture was a reality of its own, and he agreed with both Durkheim and Kroeber that the causes of culture must be sought in culture (Lowie 1917:66). These cultural antecedents could derive from both inside and outside a society, although, in the final analysis, he believed that both the inner and outer conditioning influences of a custom or artifact had to be considered. The remarkable complexity of causal factors made him look upon each culture as quite discrete and nonreplicable, but this tendency toward relativism was never strong enough to undermine his belief that the recurrence of institutions made cross-cultural comparison a profitable method. One can criticize Lowie for failing to realize that, although such practices as the use of tobacco can diffuse willy-nilly, major institutional characteristics of societies diffuse only when a basis for them has already developed. A society does not "borrow" state forms of government, for example, unless there already exists an incipient development of the state through the growth of population and social stratification. It is for this reason that, despite the skewing influences of diffusion, one may see some kind of orderly progression in the growth of social complexity and technological efficiency. But such a formulation would have breached his sense of caution, for even when he was at the point of making a broad, general statement he would pull back, hedge away. It is not his antimaterialism or his antievolutionism that explains his anthropology, for this would assume an overly idealistic interpretation of theory. Lowie's anthropology derives instead from the meticulousness of the field worker and the reserve of the man who always wore a vest and jacket.

Ideas emerge from contradiction and disputation more surely than they do from direct instruction and emulation, and it might be fair to say that Lowie was as much a student of Lewis Henry Morgan as of Franz Boas. His antievolutionary writings did much to maintain interest in the nineteenth-century pioneers, and, more important, they served to focus continued attention on the theoretical issues that dominated Morgan's writings. The evolutionists raised a number of problems that Lowie pursued. Morgan and Maine both wrote of the transition from simple societies based upon ties of kinship to civil polities based upon contractual relationships and territoriality. These were predominant concerns of Lowie also, as were the questions posed by associations and sodalities not founded on kinship lines—themes which he found in the work of the German ethnologist Heinrich Schurtz. These interests coalesced with his research on Plains Indian associations, culminating in his book, *The Origin of the State* (1927), which was one more facet of his dialogue with the evolutionists. Lowie always seemed to return to Morgan, whose main focus in his theory of evolution and chief reason for a continuing importance was the study of kinship. It is here that Morgan's influence, whether positive or negative, upon Lowie can be most clearly seen.

Morgan, as we have noted, was the first anthropologist to draw systematic attention to the study of kinship nomenclature, although he was by no means the first to recognize kinship and the forms of descent as critical features of primitive societies. It should be noted, however, that few of Morgan's contemporaries picked up the leads given by him in *Systems of Consanguinity and Affinity of the Human Family* (1871), for the most substantial additions to the theory were not made until the first two decades of the twentieth century, by W. H. R. Rivers in England and Robert Lowie in the United States. The study of kinship terms begun by Morgan was placed by Lowie and Rivers on a systematic, scientific basis that made it the principal idiom in which anthropological theories have been couched.

In order to understand the significance of kinship terms in anthropology, it is necessary to return attention to questions already touched upon in our discussion of Lowie on evolution. Kinship terminology is hardly the crux of any society, and there are many other items of far greater significance in the formation of social systems. Anthropological obsession with the subject is not, however, simply a symptom of the scholar's love of trivia, for kinship studies bring out the underlying premises of anthropological methods and the unstated assumptions in anthropological theories. Anthropologists study cultures that through the circumstances of history have undergone remarkable proliferation and differentiation, making the discipline appear to be dedicated to the exotic and the different. But, as in all the social sciences, underlying the enterprise is the belief that history is not a total jumble, a quixotic result of accident, but rather the determined outcome of certain processes. Where determination exists according to some inherent principles of order, we would expect that like factors will produce like results, just as dissimilar factors will produce divergence.

This is exactly what we find in the crosscultural study of society, for within the great variation in human custom, certain institutions and traits appear and reappear. We might be skeptical of such recurrences, as was Lowie, and attribute them to the continual borrowing of cultural items that is so constant a feature of societies having contact with one another. Indeed, it was Lowie's preference for the diffusionist explanation that made his theories so particularistic and dampened his own announced search for general laws of culture. Lowie recognized, however, that kinship and many other cultural characteristics cannot be attributed solely to borrowings, and he understood thoroughly that diffusion can be adduced only where there exists, or existed in the past, some degree of geographic proximity. Thus, he found that the similarity of tales from Tierra del Fuego and the Great Basin on the origin of man's need to work were the result of a historic connection. But he would hardly have found a connection with the Hebrew Book of Genesis; the thematic similarities were too vague and general, and the distances between the ancient Near East and the New World were too great. One may say that Lowie leaned toward the diffusionist explanation—usually not a complete explanation in any event—too heavily, but he did not do so exclusively. And in the realm of kinship terms, recurrence of features was so common and appeared in such widely separated locales that historic derivation was hardly a viable answer.

The Social Theorist

Morgan's initial survey of kinship terms revealed that, variable though the words used to classify kinsmen may be, the classifications themselves fall into a limited number of types. Most importantly, some systems completely separate lineal relatives, such as parents, children, and siblings, from collateral relatives, including aunts and uncles, cousins, nieces, and nephews, while others merge them in varying ways. Morgan referred to the former as "descriptive" systems and to the latter as "classificatory." He believed that these systems revealed either present or past patterns of mating, leading him, as we have seen, to find group marriage of siblings in the evidence of nomenclature that referred to all relatives on the first ascending generation as "father" and "mother." Moreover, it will be remembered, Morgan believed that kin terms were relatively inflexible and unchangeable, and when two societies were found with the same systems, he thought them to have once had a common identity. In this way, his evolutionism was mixed with bizarre diffusionism and hypothetical reconstructions of ancient migrations.

Lowie rejected Morgan's evolutionary scheme and his faith in the tenacity of kin terms but adhered largely to his typology and to the belief that the systems were indeed important. He had begun his publications on social organization, in general, in his early monographs, and began to organize his critique of Morgan with the publication of "Social Organization" in the *American Journal of Sociology* (1914c). In the following year, he published two articles, both entitled "Exogamy and the Classificatory Systems of Relationship" in the *American Anthropologist* and *Proceedings of the National Academy of Sciences* respectively (1915a and 1915b), which proved to be of signal importance in a major controversy that was then being waged between Rivers and Kroeber on the significance of kinship terms.[1] Rivers, in a paper entitled "On the Origin of the Classificatory System of Relationships" (Rivers 1907; cf. 1914), sided with both Edward B. Tylor and James Frazier in relating

---

[1] Although bearing the same title, the articles differed in both length and coverage. The nub of the argument is concisely stated in a paper presented before the National Academy of Sciences (1915b), and it is this version which is reprinted elsewhere in this volume (see pp. 124–28).

classificatory nomenclatures to social groups practicing exogamy. Rivers thus attempted to demonstrate the close connection between the universe of categories and classification expressed in language and the realities of social life. Indeed, this constant attempt to see the institutional basis of culture came to characterize what later became known as "British social anthropology."

Kroeber responded to the Rivers position in his paper "Classificatory Systems of Relationship" (1909), which took the stand that kinship terms could not simply be assumed to have social referents and that such conclusions could only be drawn with caution. This was hardly an argumentative position, but Kroeber went on to say that the nomenclature was more representative of the psychology of the subjects than of their social practices. It is difficult to determine what Kroeber meant by this, for it is evident that any system of conceptualization involves the mental processes of the subjects. One should ask, perhaps, how the mind draws upon the divisions of the environment for its categories, which was Emile Durkheim's procedure in *The Elementary Forms of the Religious Life* (Durkheim 1915). Or, as A. R. Radcliffe-Brown noted in 1941 (1952:61), would not one expect that there should be a congruence between the way people think of kinsmen in nomenclatural terms and the way they think of them in institutional terms? Kroeber's argument suffers further from a total misinterpretation of what Morgan meant by a classificatory system. He assumed that it referred to any lumping of kinsmen, as in the case of the English term cousin, which encompasses relatives of several genealogical positions. Of course, "cousin" is an eminently descriptive term because it totally isolates collateral relatives from the brother and sister and thus stresses the distinctive boundaries of the nuclear family. The important part of Kroeber's paper proved ultimately to be a section in which he outlined a series of eight forms of binary distinction that may be made between kinsmen in any nomenclatural system. These involved differences of generation, sex of the speaker, sex of the linking relative, sex of the relative, and so forth. The combination of such distinctions—and whether or not they are made—would yield the over-all configuration of the system. Kroeber's

The Social Theorist

scheme became the model almost fifty years later of what has become known as "componential analysis" and "ethnoscience," but it failed as a critique of Rivers's theory.

Lowie's position on the classificatory systems was much closer to that of Rivers than to Kroeber, whom he politely dismissed with faint praise. He agreed with the theory that there was indeed a connection between exogamic kin groups and classification of kin, and took care to note that Morgan had come close to saying this himself. Lowie found fault with Rivers, however, on the grounds that he had not followed his own hypothesis with sufficient rigor and was wont to cast about for alternate or supplementary explanations when faced with a seemingly impenetrable problem. Rivers's explanation fitted most neatly with the facts of the Iroquois type kinship nomenclature, or what Morgan had called the Turanian system (see Figure 1, p. 63). These systems dichotomize the kinship universe into two categories, into one of which one may marry while the other is forbidden. On the parental generation, the father's brother is merged with the father and the mother's sister with the mother, but the father's sister and mother's brother are given different terms. On a person's own generation, the children of all those kin termed father and mother are called brother and sister and fall into a class within which marriage is proscribed. On the other hand, children of the father's sister and mother's brother—called cross-cousins by anthropologists—are given a separate term and are marriageable. A fast calculation will show that wherever unilineal descent is present, whether it is patrilineal or matrilineal, the cross-cousins will always fall outside one's own descent group, although the parallel cousins, or those called brother and sister, may possibly be members of one's own group. Persons termed brother and sister are therefore not allowed to mate, but those called cousin are either preferred or at least allowed to marry. The classificatory system thus fits both unilineal and exogamous kin groups.

Lowie followed Rivers thus far but balked at Rivers's insistence that generation differences between kinsmen are so universally observed that a special explanation is needed where merging of generations occurs. At this point, Rivers attempted to explain the over-

Robert H. Lowie

riding of the generation principle by citing special customs that allowed intergenerational marriage. Lowie was on familiar ethnographic territory here, for he had studied two groups, the Crow and the Hopi, in which such merging of generations was an integral part of the kinship systems. Indeed, the Crow are the type case for the matrilineal version of such systems, whereas the Omaha are their patrilineal counterparts. The distinguishing feature of Crow kinship is the skewing of generation lines in such a way that the children of the father's sister are called father and father's sister, as are the children of the father's sister's daughter. On the mother's side, the mother's brother is called elder brother and his children are called son and daughter. There are thus no distinctive cross-cousin terms: the patrilateral cross-cousins are identified with the senior generation and the matrilateral cross-cousins are classed with the junior generation (see Figure 2).

Lowie examined Rivers's special explanation of Crow terminology, which attributed the equation of the mother's brother's children with one's own son and daughter to a practice of marrying the mother's brother's widow (and thus becoming the foster father of the deceased uncle's children), and he found it wanting. It did not explain all aspects of the system; and even worse to Lowie the methodologist, it violated the principle that "hypothetical causes shall not be multiplied unnecessarily" (Lowie 1915a:236). Lowie went on to show that matrilineal clanship, which is present among the Crow, the Hopi, and most societies which have Crow kinship, is the governing cause of the peculiarity. Thus, among the matrilineal Crow, a man belongs to the same clan as his mother's brother and is, therefore, his clan brother. He addresses him, according to this logic, by the elder brother term. Since the children of a man's true brother are called son and daughter among the Crow (and among most groups with classificatory kinship), it follows then that children of a classificatory brother will be called son and daughter. So much for the maternal side. On the father's side of the family, it must be noted that, with matrilineal clans, the father belongs to the same clan as the father's sister, as do the father's sister's children and the children of the father's sister's daughter and so on down the line. "Father"

The Social Theorist

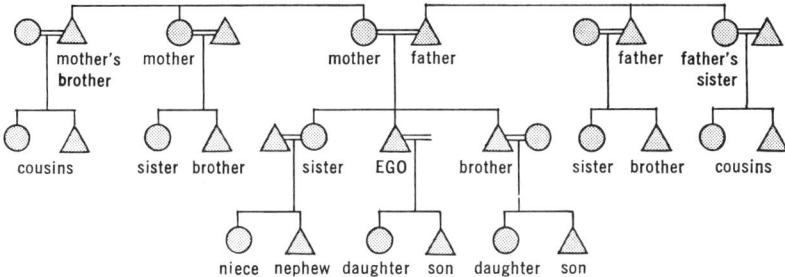

FIGURE 1. *Iroquois kinship system, male EGO as point of reference. Triangles denote males, circles females. Vertical lines show filiation; single horizontal lines indicate a sibling bond; double horizontal lines symbolize a marital union*

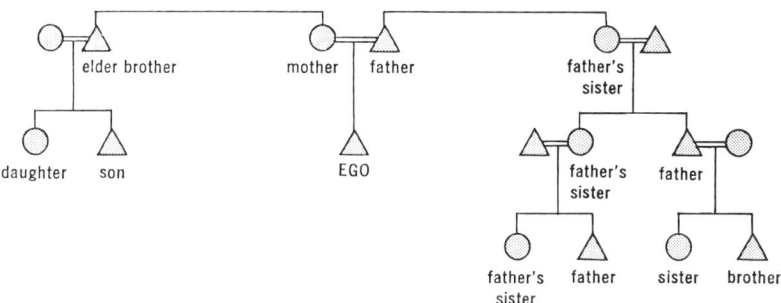

FIGURE 2. *Key elements of Crow kinship system, male EGO as point of reference*

and "father's sister" thus really mean male and female members, respectively, of one's father's clan.

Clanship effectively accounted for all the distinguishing features of the system, according to Lowie, making it unnecessary to look for extraneous factors to explain seeming anomalies. His conclusions departed from Rivers's theory by stressing social groups over exogamy and by showing that specific marriage forms were not necessarily determinative of terminology. In so doing, he augmented his attack on Morgan, for the dependency of kinship nomenclature on past or present marital practices was, of course, the essential element in Morgan's system. Lowie's reliance upon a single explanation of anything is rather surprising in view of his essentially pluralistic outlook on cultural causality and his over-all caution about generalizations of any kind. But he had not become a monist by any means. He expectedly hedged his position in 1916, the year after the publication of his papers on the classificatory system, by pointing to the influence of diffusion upon kinship terminology, reiterating his faith "that every ethnological problem is primarily a problem of distribution" (Lowie 1916:300). And in 1917, his "The Kinship Systems of the Crow and Hidatsa" (Lowie 1917b) undertook to show that the minor differences between the two systems could be attributed to linguistic factors. It was almost as if he had become alarmed by his own intrepidity. Caution won the day, as it nearly always did with Lowie.

Lowie's work on kinship hardly ended with his analysis of the Crow and Omaha systems, but it exemplifies his method and theories better than most of his subsequent publications. He eschewed the dogmatism of Rivers, and later that of Radcliffe-Brown, who assumed that terminology always reflected social reality, faithfully and point by point. The empirical evidence accumulated in the intervening decades shows that kinship systems may have, to the contrary, a relationship to social groups quite different from neat isomorphism, and that the terms must always be studied in the light of concrete behavior. Lowie's skepticism was well placed, but he nonetheless established an American tradition in the study of social organization that required conceptual schemes, such as kinship terminology, to be seen in the context of the sociology of the people. This is a view that is commonly attributed to Radcliffe-Brown, whose well-known article on Crow and Omaha kinship, "The Study of Kinship Systems," did not appear, however, until twenty-six years after Lowie's papers on classificatory systems. Radcliffe-Brown added little to Lowie, and it is all the more remarkable that his entire essay never mentioned the Lowie work on which it was ultimately based.

Lowie's work on kinship groups and terms did much to destroy

The Social Theorist

Morgan's *Ancient Society* while celebrating his *Systems of Consanguinity and Affinity of the Human Family*. In the first place a negative task of sweeping away what he believed to be intellectual debris, Lowie's final contribution was lasting and positive. Despite the common view that Lowie was a "historical particularist" who viewed culture as "a thing of shreds and patches," he actually was a forerunner of functionalist theory in this country. His early work on kinship predated the publications of Malinowski and the theoretical writings of Radcliffe-Brown, and his criticism of Morgan rested heavily on Morgan's failure to see facts in a contemporary relationship to each other. And, although it is well remembered that the great British functionalists were scathing in their denunciation of historical reconstructions, or "conjectural history," based upon alleged "survivals" of earlier stages of history, Lowie led the way in his attack upon Morgan's notion that kinship nomenclatures were, in themselves, survivals. He showed them, instead, to be living and vital parts of social organisms. But he was a cautious functionalist, whose aims were also historical. Writing in another context of his Crow kinship research, he said:

> ✤ *My instances show, then, that culture traits may be functionally related, and this fact renders possible a parallelism, however limited, of cultural developments in different parts of the globe. The field of culture, then, is not a region of complete lawlessness* (Lowie 1917a:88).

Lowie searched for relationships, and he saw such links to be, in the final analysis, the results of similar historical causes, as verifiable by the comparative method. His kinship work encapsulated what were to become the major orientations of American anthropology, a point to which we will return in our conclusions.

Lowie is best known for his publications on kinship, but he was also a student of social organization in the broadest sense. The collective aggregates of society, whether clans, moieties, clubs, governments, or sects—all fell within his purview. As Lowie was a student of primitive societies, the institutions of kinship loomed large in his work. But he never fell into the trap of becoming a "kinship man," as have many anthropologists who have found in kinship studies a tidy and orderly retreat in a disconcertingly diffuse field. Although a man of Lowie's personality must have found great satisfaction in the manipulation of ego charts and the search for regular recurrences of nomenclatural peculiarities, he would not have been able to abide the recent style, which he found wanting in Kroeber so long ago, of looking upon kinship as a closed cognitive domain. Kinship, as part of social life, had to relate to the totality of social life—and in this sense Lowie was indeed a functionalist by orientation, however limited his conclusions.

It was this concern for the totality of social organization that brought him into the study of political institutions. There were other motives as well, for Lowie's relentless pursuit of the unilinear evolutionists forced him to confront their ideas on the origin of the state and civil society. Morgan had traced the growth of the civil order out of clanship to the rise of private property, undoubtedly the one salient point in his theory that attracted the attention of Marx and Engels. Whereas past polities had been inextricably part of clan organization, the new form of the state, according to Morgan, was based upon a territorial principle. This was not at all an original idea, for Sir Henry Maine, the great pioneer of comparative jurisprudence, had come to much the same conclusions some sixteen years before Morgan. In his *Ancient Law* (1861), Maine found the legal basis of primitive societies to be founded on ties of blood, which bestowed membership in kinship units and allocation of kinship roles as a function of birth. This social position of the primitive man was said to be founded on status, or what we would call today "ascription," as contrasted to the position of man vis-à-vis society in more advanced polities. States, conversely, are based mainly upon the factor of physical contiguity, or territory, and the principal mode of establishing social relations within them is by contract under a system of codified laws. In primitive societies, a man is born to a certain status and to membership in a kin group or tribe that provides him with his social identity and effectively and legitimately exercises social control over him. In the state, a man's position is determined by legally binding agreements into which he has entered; his membership in a political group, or at least the propriety of its control over his activities, is an outcome of the fact that he is within its territory.

Lowie took no great issue with this important, and still valid, distinction between the tribe and the state. He objected, however, to the view, which he attributed to Morgan and Maine, that territorial and contractual ties were unique to the state, a new and emergent kind of social relationship that had not existed before in the history of man. Lowie was actually a great admirer of Maine's work, and in *The History of Ethnological Theory* (Lowie 1937:51) showed his theories to be quite different from unilinear evolutionism. But on this one issue he found fault and proceeded in a number of works to point to the existence of territorial and other nonkinship institutions in primitive societies. His interest in this area developed easily out of his studies of Plains Indians, just as his kinship work found fertile soil in his ethnography, for many of the Plains groups had associations in which membership was not based on kinship. These organizations, or sodalities, exercised coercive power, including the right to invoke physical sanctions over members of the tribes during certain periods and for certain reasons. They thus conformed in part to Lowie's definition of the state: "The state, then, embraces the inhabitants of a definite area who acknowledge the legitimacy of force when applied by the individuals whom they accept as rulers or governors" (Lowie 1948a:317).

Lowie's three criteria of the state—territoriality, legitimacy, and monopoly of violence—are close to Max Weber's definition, as well as to Maine's. The relevance of the Plains Indians to such a view of the civil order derives from the fact that among many Plains tribes there existed sodalities that functioned as military organizations in time of war and as regulators of activity in large encampments and in migration during times of peace. Most notably, the military sodalities had the specific duty of maintaining order and discipline during the great annual buffalo hunts. The hunt was preeminently a group activity in which large bands of hunters mounted on specially trained horses sought to surround the herds or to kill off the animals as they stampeded. A lone hunter could well run off a herd of thousands while killing only one buffalo. Such individual enterprise was universally disapproved on the Plains, but among many of the groups the military societies were given the responsibility of policing the camp and forcibly preventing infractions. A lone hunter could be severely beaten, his weapons destroyed, and his horse killed. Here, certainly, was a case of the legitimate use of violence, which Lowie thought was a parallel of state controls.

The question of whether these sodalities had a "territorial" base, however, is a knotty one. Membership in the societies was obtained by various means, but generally not according to kinship criteria. Lowie went to great pains to show the variability of recruitment procedures, which, however, if not by kinship, were at least confined to the sociopolitical unit, or tribe. And tribal membership was largely a result of birth and not a question of presence in a delimited and legally circumscribed territory. Indeed, the Plains groups were highly nomadic, and frontiers between groups were, at best, amorphous and shifting. Primitive societies occupy physical space, of course, but this is hardly territoriality as understood in the concept of the state, a point that Morton Fried has made in a passage critical of Lowie (Fried 1967:46). The essence of the territoriality of the state consists in the continual application of governing control over an area in which the population may well be, and usually is, culturally heterogeneous; and such conditions were not found on the Plains. But, in all fairness to Lowie, he saw only the possible germs of the state in such organizations. His position on the matter actually vacillated, for in *Primitive Society* he saw sodalities, in general, as "potential agencies for the creation of a state by uniting the population within a circumscribed area into an aggregate that functions as a definite unit irrespective of other social affiliations of the inhabitants" (Lowie 1920:395). But Lowie was always powerfully impressed by the ethnographic exceptions to the best of generalizations and seven years later, in *The Origin of the State* (1927), he wrote that "associations are not inherently either centralizing or disruptive agencies" (Lowie 1927:111). Even later, however, having reached a stage of mellowness that allowed for venture, Lowie stated what probably best summarizes his view of the relation between associations and civil society:

> *I still feel that the military organizations of the Plains area exemplify the potentialities of associations as regards the creation of supreme central authority. It is merely necessary to remember that such germs of statehood actually as a rule remained rudimentary (Lowie 1943:70).*

Lowie's concern with associations had other roots in evolutionary theory than the work of Maine and Morgan. He was apparently one of the few anthropologists of his time, at least in this country, who had read Heinrich Schurtz's *Alterklassen und Männerbünde* (Age Classes and Men's Clubs, 1902), which projected an evolutionary development of associations from age classes into men's ranked societies. Lowie found in Schurtz a refutation of Morgan's view that the clan was the distinguishing feature of primitive political organization, but he devoted long sections of *Primitive Society* to refuting the evolutionism of the German ethnologist's theory. Expectably, he found that Schurtz's stages of development did not hold up empirically, and that the scheme had neglected the element of diffusion. The net result was that Lowie had bogged down in a welter of ethnographic minutiae any theorization on associations, but he had drawn attention to the importance of such organizations to the social systems of primitive societies. He had also rescued Schurtz and his theory from oblivion.

The attempt to stress the territorial component of primitive social organization had as much significance for the study of kinship as for politics. Indeed, it may even be argued that this was the most important contribution of *The Origin of the State*. Lowie's chapter "The Territorial Tie," reprinted further in this book (pp. 129–43), pointed again to the coexistence of ties of kinship and of neighborhood in primitive societies, although acknowledging the general ascendency of the former over the latter. But he went beyond this familiar thesis to assert that "if we inquire into the bond of consanguinity itself, we find lurking in the background a spatial determinant of the sentiments underlying it" (Lowie 1927:73). This is a restatement of Lowie's already-mentioned position that residential arrangements are prior to, and possibly causal of, kinship alignments, a thesis which he developed in *Primitive Society* while demonstrating the possibilities for independent and diverse origins of clanship.

According to Lowie, Tylor actually provided the essential clue to the residential basis of kinship in his essay "The Matrilineal Family System" (1896). Here, Tylor showed that kinship sentiments become skewed by the factor of coresidence. Thus, in a matrilocal household, a child would grow up on close terms with his maternal aunt but would remain removed from the paternal aunt. Much the same line of reasoning informed Tylor in his classic essay "On a Method of Investigating the Development of Institutions" (1889), in which he showed by crude statistics that there was a correspondence between mother-in-law avoidance and matrilocality. Lowie further drew on the ethnography of the Angami Naga of the Assam Hills of India, where marriage within presumably exogamic groups occurs but never between two co-members living in the same village (Lowie 1927:62–64). Since the time he wrote this, there have been numerous other accounts of household and locality exogamy overriding the rules set by kinship; my own account of the Mundurucú prohibition of marriage between a man and his sister's daughter under modern conditions of matrilocality is but one of these (Murphy 1956).

Emphasis upon the local and spatial determinants of kinship sentiments and kinship institutions is one of Lowie's most important contributions to anthropological theory. His work indeed stressed the normative as opposed to the action elements in society, but underlying this orientation was a latent theory which had to await clear enunciation by others. He argued against strict economic determinism continually, but any systematic theory of the territorial factors he hypothesized as underlying kinship must work from technology and resources to institutional structures through the intermediary of how, where, when, and with whom people work and congregate. This is the essential method of Julian H. Steward's theory of cultural ecology (cf. Steward 1938); and Lowie's stamp upon his student is clear in Steward's assignment of priority to activity and congregation over rule and norm. If patrilineal descent is to be explained, then look for conditions that would bring together as a continuing and corporate unit a group of male kin related in the male line. This is what Lowie, in effect, stated, but that he did not delve into the spatial arrangements to seek out their ecological determinants was a weakness in his work, which he confessed to freely.

In his publications on political organization, it would appear at first reading that Lowie is tearing everything apart with data and negative example. But a second and a third reading show that he was always putting things back together as well, although in a different way. His work on the state explicitly set out to show a continuity and a unity between primitive and state societies—that as kinship persists in the state so does neighborliness originate in primitive life. To Lowie, this was one more manifestation of psychic unity and the commonality of the human experience. Beyond this, his critical bent cut through such clichéd categories as consanguinity and locality to show that they were not simple, one-sided, and isolated phenomena but were indeed totally intertwined. The anthropology of his time regarded primitives as either anarchic or totally governed by clan life, or at least by kinship. Lowie tried to show that law and government, however attenuated in form, were general in human society. Typically, he came to no firm conclusions on the origin of the state or of civil society, but he laid out the arguments for those who would follow him.

The bulk of Lowie's writings were clearly concerned with the sphere of social institutions and units; he left no doubt that he dealt on the analytic level of culture, and it was within the realm of social activity and culture that he sought, however tentatively, the causes or determinants of culture. It would seem inconsistent, then, that Lowie should announce his lifelong interest in psychology and proclaim his writings to have been influenced by that discipline. Lowie's psychology, however, was learned at Columbia, and the experimental behaviorism that was then being established in its new department no doubt appealed greatly to the young student of Mach and Haeckel. Whatever the attraction, Lowie added associational learning theory to his intellectual equipment instead of the depth psychology that was then being developed in his native Vienna. And it was behavioristic psychology, in all of its pale mechanism, that influenced his *Primitive Religion* (1924), his one major venture into psychological concerns.

Religion was an abiding interest in Lowie's ethnography, and his early writings number many articles as well as more substantial works on mythology, ceremonialism, and belief systems. His own background in scientific agnosticism brought him to the field with at least an open mind on the subject, but his experiences among North American Indians and Christian missionaries convinced him of the procrustean nature of the religious sentiment and of its basic function in endowing life with meaning and culture with unity. His attitude toward religion, he said, was that of the scientist. There is no need for any essential conflict between science and religion, as each deals with different realms: science seeks truth incompletely, and religion offers false truths absolutely. Neither is a substitute for the other. The attitude of the scientist toward religion must be one of objectivity, his role to study and not to judge or evaluate. He agreed with Durkheim that religious notions were no less real for being chimerical, for, to the extent that they influenced behavior and helped mold culture, religious phenomena had substance. The scientist, then, must evaluate the meaning of religion to its practitioners, however irrational the beliefs and practices may seem to the observer.

One aspect of Lowie's "psychological" approach to religion derived from his attempt to understand its subjective meaning to the believer, for the sense of awe, wonder, and mystery was, for him, one of the defining criteria of the religious experience. Another root of his psychological orientation was his view that the religious experience is a profoundly individual one, shaped, defined, and articulated, though it is, by culture. He took Durkheim to task for his derivation of the origin of religion from the social group and its constraints. His treatment of Durkheim's work was shallow, and managed to reduce

The Social Theorist

most of the great French sociologist's arguments to banalities. But Lowie's own bent for viewing religion as a system of subjective meanings that somehow or other give individual satisfaction becomes clear in his discussion. He made much of the fact that ceremonial congregations, so important in Durkheim's theory, were not an essential element in Plains Indian religions, where the individual vision quest and communication with individual guardian spirits were focal points of the religious life. The content of the vision quests was derived largely from culture, but the impetus was not.

Lowie's approach to religion is perhaps best exemplified by his chapter "Association" in *Primitive Religion*. This section is concerned ultimately with the process of how certain signs become associated with a sense of the "Extraordinary" and thus become part of religious symbolism. Lowie found that to a large extent the prior cultural milieu was the essential conditioning factor, and this element was invoked to explain how certain borrowed traits become incorporated into a religious complex and endowed with a sense of wonder. He could not break out of his historicism.

The main problem with Lowie's work on religion is that, in common with William James, whom he so admired, he never says what the roots of the Extraordinary are; there is no unifying theory of religion. Freud does not even appear in his bibliography, and his references to psychoanalytic interpretations are usually poorly informed and reduced to a determinism of "the sex instincts." Revealingly, his discussion of "the view that religion is at bottom nothing but misunderstood erotic emotions" (Lowie 1948b:218) occurs in the chapter entitled "Women and Religion." *Primitive Religion* was severely criticized by Radin, Goldenweiser, and others among his old friends and colleagues, and their barbs apparently hurt. But their criticisms were well taken, for *Primitive Religion* is probably the least valuable of Lowie's books. Although stressing the subjective aspects of religious experience, he failed to reach below surface appearances. The study of religion was reduced to its phenomenology, and the psychological framework was adequate only for a treatment of the mechanics of diffusion and reintegration of religious traits. One of the great disappointments of the book, given Lowie's prowess in the field of social organization, is that in his haste to discredit Durkheim he abstracted and severed religion from the totality of social life.

The weaknesses of *Primitive Religion* reflect certain of the weaknesses of Lowie as an anthropologist. His rigid scientism, a view of method that was better adapted to the study of matter than of man, produced an empiricism that stifled generalizations, and sometimes even thought. Arguments frequently became lost in a welter of facts piled upon facts without selection and restraint. He used data as a control over generalizations, which is how an anthropologist should operate. But every time he neared a conclusion, he would couch his results in a series of cautions and exceptions. Lowie did not really believe that one exception disproved a rule, but he certainly thought that it beclouded it sufficiently to warrant a very careful circumscription of the generalization. In a way, he expected too much of his material. If there is law in culture and history, it is probabilistic in nature. But Lowie's scientific universe was a mechanical one which did not allow for vagary and fluidity. The tidiness of his world view thus produced a looseness of results, for he overlooked order by his insistence that there should be more.

There is a paradox in the methodological aspect of Lowie's work, but there is further paradox in his theories. Lowie inveighed at length against economic determinism, as well as evolutionism. But just as he did much to perpetuate interest in the evolutionists, so also did he lay groundwork for a new "materialism." While Kroeber's anthropology was taking him further into the realm of pattern and idea, Lowie confined himself largely to the more concrete area of social groups and relationships, an area in which he established the principle that one must look to the physical arrangements of a society to understand the ideal categories by which it sees itself. That he did not follow up these leads himself is a great pity, but such a venture would certainly have tried his abhorrence of generalization. It was left to Julian Steward and others to follow Lowie's work through to its logical conclusions and to fill in the areas that he had left vacant.

The Social Theorist

Robert Lowie did much to give American anthropology its direction and flavor, although it is not possible to point to any nexus of consistent theory or viewpoint that is distinctive of his work. Indeed, it is perhaps this diffuseness and lack of theoretical unity that make him, in retrospect, the most important American anthropologist of his time, for these are characteristics of the discipline itself in this country. But beyond this rather negative affinity, Lowie's work bespoke trends that have become established in the profession. He was a functionalist who did not believe in the universalism of function, but who saw in regularly recurrent social characteristics the possibility of teasing out correlations with other institutions and thus deriving laws of limited scope. Despite the virulence of his earlier antievolutionism, he groped hesitantly toward formulating less ambitious developmental sequences that would perhaps have applicability to an area, if not a world. It was Lowie who coined the term "multilinear evolution" (Lowie 1948:33 ff.) to refer to the possibility that there may have been several evolutionary sequences in the development of social life. And it was his student Steward who developed the bare idea into a theory (Steward 1955). Finally, Lowie's concern with history has been also an abiding characteristic of American anthropology, whether pursued in the metier of culture history, diffusion studies, archeology, or as ethnohistory. Lowie's fault was that he did not adequately account for the evident premise that the same factors that made a proffered cultural trait acceptable and desirable, or at least assimilable, could also lead to the independent invention of something very much like it. Most anthropologists today would agree that diffusion does not throw off the order of history as much as Lowie believed. But then Lowie was actually a moderate diffusionist as compared to his contemporaries.

Lowie was first, last, and always a scientist, and if this has made his work less exciting to many, his ideas less grand, such is the price that must be paid for his kind of empiricism. But it had very positive features as well. Lowie tore apart a good deal that needed tearing apart, for he disassembled words and classifications that had become hardened into immutable realities. He took the notion of clanship, as received from the nineteenth century, and, stripping away its mystique, proceeded to show the remarkable variability hidden within. This did not make *Primitive Society* exciting reading, but after the initial adverse reactions, it eventually enabled anthropologists to think more clearly of the nature of descent groups. This was often so with Lowie, leading to the erroneous impression that his was a negative approach. He destroyed edifices, but edifices are composed of walls that imprison as well as shelter. Claude Lévi-Strauss writes in *Tristes Tropiques* that reading *Primitive Society* liberated him from an overburden of academic philosophy:

> But instead of notions borrowed from books and at once metamorphosed into philosophical concepts I was confronted with an account of first-hand experience. The observor, moreover, had been so committed as to keep intact the full meeting of his experience. My mind escaped from the closed circuit which was what the practice of academic philosophy amounted to: made free to the open air, it breathed deeply and took on new strength. Like a townsman let loose in the mountains, I made myself drunk with the open spaces and my astonished eye could hardly take in the wealth and variety of the scene (Lévi-Strauss 1963:63).

Robert H. Lowie reopened issues that had become closed or obscured, and he reopened them with the wealth of unique experience, the knowledge of the richness of the universe of society, that can come only through the ethnographic experience. He left behind him a legacy of discipline and control, a penchant for questioning and requestioning, an attitude of skepticism that are the hallmarks of a discipline. He was a professional.

PART II

Selected Writings of Robert H. Lowie

    Lowie was an inveterate and fascinating raconteur of things past, and the reminiscences of the following article present a tapestry of the entire intellectual climate in which Lowie and his fellow students were reared (see also text, pp. 11–14). Although written late in Lowie's life, it is an appropriate first reading of the man, for he gathers in these pages all the strands which influenced him. The reader finds anthropology at its nascency, at a time when there were only three academic departments of anthropology and but a handful of professors in the subject. Lowie lived through a period that saw scores of universities embark upon graduate programs in anthropology, and the number of fellows of the American Anthropological Association exceed one thousand. It was a time of building of departments and programs and of the formulation of a distinctive discipline and method.

    Of special interest are Lowie's comments on the disillusionment with evolutionism and the rise of a critical empiricism that was influenced just as much by the growing tradition of ethnographic

Robert H. Lowie

field work as by European inductive science. Lowie also describes the influences upon anthropology of the new psychologies that were emerging at the time; and he speaks, correctly, of the period as one of epistemological revolution. The students of the time shredded the neat categories received from the past into their component parts and rearranged them in different ways to better understand the reality behind them. "We had learned to view catchwords with suspicion," said Lowie.

Reminiscences of Anthropological Currents in America Half a Century Ago *

✤ The Editor of the AMERICAN ANTHROPOLOGIST has asked me to offer "some discussion and analysis of the intellectual ferment, the various ideas and interests, and the important factual discoveries in their relationship to these ideas, that were current during the period of your early years as an anthropologist." In responding I shall have to go far afield. The task suggested implies nevertheless two noteworthy restrictions. Factual discoveries are irrelevant (except as they influenced ideas), as is administrative promotion of scientific interests. Accordingly, though sharing Sapir's judgment that as a field worker J. O. Dorsey was "ahead of his age," I must ignore him for present purposes. Again, there will be only brief references to Frederic Ward Putnam (1839–1915) and to Frederic Webb Hodge (1864–1956); as to Powell and McGee, only their thinking demands extended notice.

It is well to recall that in 1904, when I began graduate work, only Columbia, Harvard, and California had full-fledged academic departments of anthropology, but the Field Museum, a descendant of the Chicago World's Fair of 1893, had been fostering research, as had the Bureau of American Ethnology and the United States National Museum. The anthropological departments of Columbia and of the American Museum of Natural History were still intimately con-

* Reproduced by permission of the American Anthropological Association from *American Anthropologist*, Vol. 58, no. 6, pp. 995–1016, 1956.

Selected Writings

nected; even closer was the bond between the Museum of Anthropology in San Francisco and the department in Berkeley, both of them being parts of the University of California. Thus, New York, Washington, Chicago, and San Francisco-Berkeley were the chief centers of anthropological activity.

If the following pages seem to give disproportionate mention of my own university, this is not due to parochialism on my part. In 1904 Columbia indisputably provided the most comprehensive training to be obtained in the country. My first seminar there was attended by Alfred M. Tozzer, already a Ph.D. from Harvard. When John R. Swanton had presented a linguistic dissertation at Harvard, the Columbia professor was invited to examine him. Before George A. Dorsey sent Fay-Cooper Cole to the Philippines, he had him spend a semester with Boas, and after his return from the field Cole returned to take his degree in New York.

In the present essay I shall begin by sketching the orientation of men whose thinking developed independently of this particular academic tradition. I shall then attempt to indicate the intellectual movements that impinged on my generation and presumably in large measure on our teachers'. It is hardly necessary to emphasize that even among the small number of prospective professionals at the time the reactions to these impulses varied considerably, in accordance with our greatly varying individualities and equally diverse backgrounds.

I

Whatever may be said in criticism of the scholars to be treated in this section, they numbered among them men of unquestionable talent and enthusiasm. As will be shown, some were unusual personalities, some achieved important scientific results. It is my considered opinion that the less impressive individualities among them did the most useful and most lasting work.

Cushing (1857–1900). During one of my seminars the name of Frank Hamilton Cushing happened to come up. "He was an exceedingly able man," Boas declared. Then he paused. After a brief intermission he resumed: "I'm afraid his work will have to be done all over again."

To a novice the judgment seemed a curious *non sequitur*. Had I known Cushing's writings, I could have filled in the ellipse. Cushing *was* exceedingly able: with rare manual skill he could duplicate aboriginal artifacts; and with rare perceptiveness he recorded elusive Indian usages. But his was an undisciplined imagination; he was able to impart the flavor of the Pueblo atmosphere, but he leaves us wondering how much of his interpretation reflects his own rather than his native hosts' mentality (Cushing [1884-85] 1920). A sober inquirer of later date found his versions of Zuñi myth highly suspect; for the most part "the endless poetic and metaphysic glossing of the basic elements" probably "originated in Cushing's own mind" (Bunzel 1932:547 f.).

The one general principle of interpretation Cushing used was evolution, linked with the doctrine of psychic unity. Culture is due "chiefly to the necessities encountered during its development." Nothing seemed more natural than that the ancestral Pueblo entering the Southwest first used gourds and baskets, then by their unaided efforts achieved pottery. Cushing expresses his indebtedness to E. B. Tylor, yet a vital phase of the British anthropologist's thinking eluded him. For Tylor expressly notes the continuous distribution of ceramics in North America from Mexico northward, inferring that the art "spread from a single source" (Tylor, 1865:3). Indeed, Cushing conceived the whole of Pueblo culture as a spontaneous local growth: people driven into the Southwest at first subsisted on roots and seeds until they were "spurred on by that great motor of humanity—hunger—to a knowledge of irrigation and horticulture" (Cushing 1920:516 f.). Correspondingly, they began by constructing brush lodges, but "by a series of stages" advanced "to the recent and present terraced, many storied, ceremonial structures" (Cushing 1886:473–81).

It is not surprising that at the World's Fair in Chicago Cushing argued against any evidence for ancient cultural contact between the New World and other continents (Holmes 1893:425 f.).

Brinton (1837-1899). Among the eminent men of his period, Daniel Garrison Brinton was not the least remarkable; and like Cushing he was an uncompromising champion of unilinear evolution. Among his American contemporaries he stands out in several ways. Though, unlike the rest, he did no field work, his reading covered the whole range of our science. Medically trained, he sometimes dealt with physical anthropology, but his greatest effort went into ethnological linguistics, mythology, and comparative religion. He edited an eight-volume *Library of American Aboriginal Literature* (1882-1890). He held a chair of American Archaeology and Linguistics at the University of Pennsylvania. Attending scientific congresses, he became personally known to the leaders of the science abroad; Rudolf Virchow once asked George Grant MacCurdy to convey his regards to Brinton [oral communication of G.G.M. to R.H.L.]. Probably no American-born colleague of his generation was so deeply saturated with the European atmosphere. He had studied at Paris and Heidelberg, and profusely quoted from German, French, and Italian sources. Nor were his interests restricted to scholarship; he haunted European picture galleries, read Browning and Tennyson, admired Ibsen and Zola when their names were still anathema. Altogether he published twenty-three books and innumerable articles —on the Mound Builders, on Anthropopithecus, on the philosophy of language, on Central American guardian spirits, and what not (Smyth *et al.*, 1900).

Of the effectiveness of his teaching I have found no record, but A. B. Lewis once told me that Brinton had been a spirited debater at scientific gatherings, a statement quite credible to a reader of his reviews.

Here, then, was a man of independent mind, unusual erudition, and exceptional cultivation, yet amazingly little profit can be drawn from his writings. Of course, he was not always wrong and he helped dispel some popular fallacies, such as the existence of tribes without religion, the degraded character of African fetishism, or the racial distinctness of the Mound Builders (Brinton 1898:31, 101; 1901:255). But many of the opinions most confidently voiced by him must be read to be believed. Decades after Waitz he quotes old wives' tales about aboriginal mentality: the Australians are marked by "almost brutal stupidity"; their "natural feelings and moral perceptions seem incredibly blunted" (1898:16 f.). There are even incredible ethnographic blunders: the Melanesians, *unlike the Polynesians*, are said to be agriculturists (1901:228, 237).

Confusingly Brinton mingles racial, cultural, and linguistic points of view. One is inclined to praise him for citing types of arrow release as samples of motor habits, but alas! he seems to conceive them as biologically determined since the relevant passage occurs between a comparison of human with simian musculature and a description of steatopygy. The American Indians are characterized by copper color, straight hair, *and* incorporating languages.

Considering that he plumed himself on his linguistic insight, some pertinent thoughts of Brinton's have a curious flavor. Following Horatio Hale, he thus explains the differentiation of stocks: Children are forever coining new words and among themselves soon evolve a distinctive idiom. Barbarians would often leave very young children behind, and "those who survived developed a tongue of their own, nearly all of whose radicals would be totally different from those of the languages of their parents. Thus, in early times . . . numerous independent tongues came to be spoken within limited areas by the same ethnic stock" (Brinton 1901:33, 36 f., 61 f., 63, 65, 74 *et seq.*, 97 f., 237).

The work on *The American Race* exhibits a certain independence of Powell, e.g. in recognizing a Uto-Aztecan family, though it was left for Sapir to provide the demonstration. As a whole, the book is a sad disappointment. Brinton vehemently rejects any affinity between American Indians and the Mongoloids; the former entered the New World by a land-bridge between Europe (or "Eurafrica") and America; they "could have come from no other quarter." Within the Western Hemisphere, parallelism is carried to a ludicrous extreme. Like Cushing, Brinton regards Pueblo culture as "a local product, developed in independent tribes by the natural facilities offered by the locality. . . . The culture of the Pueblos, both ancient and modern, bears every mark of local and independent growth" (1891:17–58, 113–17, 336 f.).

Selected Writings

Consistently with this position, Brinton had interpreted the same myth even in neighboring tribes as the result of psychic unity (1868:172 f.). The "universal mythical cycles" were "independent creations of the human intellect, framed under laws common to it everywhere, and which tend always to produce fruits generically everywhere the same" (1898:117 f., 129).

It is a melancholy reflection that Brinton's enthusiasm and learning produced so slight a permanent contribution.

Powell and McGee. John Wesley Powell (1834–1902) and his collaborator William John McGee (1853–1912) are best treated jointly. In a different way from Brinton they were both remarkable men. Notwithstanding the loss of his right arm in the Civil War, Powell intrepidly achieved the descent of the Colorado River (1869, 1871); McGee, while suffering the tortures of cancer, was able to record his subjective experiences for a scientific publication. As scientists, both men were primarily geologists, but became absorbed in anthropology and strove valiantly to make it a *science*, sometimes in a rather naïve way. Characteristic is their emphasis on the biologists' principle of priority in nomenclature. I have heard McGee defend it before a session of the American Anthropological Association as though the matter were of vital importance for the status of our discipline. If a reader of the *Handbook of American Indians North of Mexico* (1907, 1910) who seeks information on the Blackfoot is referred to an article on the "Siksika," it is due to this Powellian crotchet. No less peculiar is the mania of both men for newly coined words. Their writings teem with such terms as "sophiology," "esthetology," "demonomy," "historics." Administratively they have won undying renown, Powell by founding the Bureau of American Ethnology (1879) and its series of publications, McGee both as Powell's collaborator and as the foremost organizer of the American Anthropological Association (Hodge 1912:686). But our concern is with their scientific contributions.

From that point of view we are once more doomed to disillusionment. Neither ranks high as a field investigator. Powell met many Ute and Paiute on his Far Western explorations and claimed a speaking acquaintance with their dialects, but apart from four good versions of myths (Powell 1881) and occasional tidbits, he published nothing of ethnographic value. McGee's most ambitious research project was devoted to the Seri, to whom he dedicated a 300-page treatise on the basis of little over a week's observation (McGee 1898). Kroeber, who went over the ground later, gives full credit to his predecessor's extraordinary gifts as an observer. However, McGee's uncontrolled imagination and his strong preconceptions yielded a distorted picture (Kroeber 1931:3, 18).

The intellectual set of the two men is well illustrated by their formulation and solution of a specific problem. After his brief sojourn McGee conceived the Seri as "notably egoistic and inimical toward contemporaries"; thereby they contrasted with the "notably altruistic" Papago, though both tribes share the same type of environment. Other peoples having been examined from the same point of view, the Papago stood "in the front rank of aboriginal tribes as graded by power of nature-conquest," whereas the Seri were at the opposite extreme. What conclusion is drawn from these facts? "The Seri, habitually submitting to a harsh environment . . . merely reflect its harshness in their conduct," while "the Papago, seeking habitually to control environment in the interests of their kind . . . are raised by their efforts to higher planes of humanity" (Powell 1903:XXVIII).

However, as Professor Heizer has pointed out to me, there was another side to McGee that explains the high personal regard in which he was held by such exacting judges as Boas and George A. Dorsey. When a situation fitted into his geological experience he could display exemplary caution. In Pleistocene deposits in Nevada he discovered an undeniable artifact, which a conservative archeologist (Holmes 1919:69 f.) pronounced "the second most important observation yet recorded bearing upon the problems of the high geological antiquity of man in America." But McGee himself refused to draw sensational inferences from a single find (McGee 1889), leaving the matter in abeyance. *Si ita omnia dixisset!*

To return to Powell, his one effective publication in our field is the treatise on North American linguistic stocks (Powell 1891:1–142). Acknowledging his indebtedness to other investigators, such

Selected Writings

as Gallatin, Henshaw, Pilling, Gatschet, and J. O. Dorsey, he assumed sole responsibility for the classification presented. He accepted as probable the subsequent fusion of some of his stocks, but foresaw no material reduction in the total number (1891:26 f.). Americanists have often chafed at his conservatism, but the scheme has unquestionably helped to bring order into chaos and has probably aided ethnography more than a bolder classification might have done. It is more profitable to seek cultural resemblances between Navaho and Chipewyan than between Ojibwa and Yurok.

As for their philosophy of culture, Powell and McGee fell back on evolution, perpetrating some of the dreariest series of stages ever concocted in its name. To the familiar categories of savagery, barbarism, and civilization, they added enlightenment (Powell 1888). Human thought was said to fall into two major divisions, the mythological and the scientific. Within the former there were four stages: in the beginning men assigned life to everything; next they anthropomorphized and deified beasts; then they superseded animal gods with the personified and deified natural powers (physitheism); finally they deified mental, moral, social traits, such as war, love, etc. (psychotheism).

Concerning social organization, Powell in no way advanced beyond Lewis H. Morgan. His terminological separation of unilineal descent groups into matrilineal "clans" and "patrilineal" gentes is defensible and gained a following among American scholars. In the classical tradition he assigned clans to savagery, gentes to barbarism. The change in rule of descent had several causes. For one thing, the priestly office was passed on from father to son [Why? one asks], whereby patrilineal reckoning became fundamental. Again, women were separated from their clansfolk when following their husbands to fishing and hunting grounds, by which practice the husbands' and fathers' authority was enhanced to the detriment of maternal, fraternal, and avuncular powers. Agriculture tended to influence developments in the same direction, for women and children would be working "under the immediate supervision and control of husbands and fathers." As is usual with Powell, no concrete examples are given in support of these generalizations (Powell 1896:10 f., 14 f.).

Robert H. Lowie

Adolphe Bandelier. To the foregoing galaxy of American "characters" may be added Swiss-born Adolphe Bandelier (1840–1914), an original if ever there was one. As a student in his first class at Columbia I speak from personal acquaintance. His astonishing knowledge of Latin-American sources was coupled with extravagant vehemence, obstinacy, engaging naïveté, and a bizarre sense of humor. My fellow-student Speck he addressed as "Lord Bacon." In the midst of a lecture he once stigmatized a scholar he disliked as "that damned liar, Sir Clements Markham." Seeing me in the hall outside his classroom one afternoon he approached me with an air of mystery, threw an arm around my shoulders, and confidentially asked, "Lowie, can you tell me where the toilet is?" At a social gathering in Boas' house I remember his arriving late, advancing toward his host, and truculently remarking, "*Meine Frau lässt Sie nicht grüssen.*" Then, turning to Mrs. Boas, he said, "*Meine Frau lässt Sie beinahe grüssen.*" [The humor of this is lost in English. R.F.M.]

Bandelier did do significant field work in the Eastern Pueblos, in Mexico, and in the Andes. He is especially noted, however, for the effective demolition of the widespread belief in grandiose American empires, though he considerably overshot the mark. As a theorist, he ranks admittedly as a satellite of Lewis H. Morgan (Bandelier 1877, 1878, 1879). With admirable cogency Professor Leslie White has demonstrated how Bandelier, modifying his original conceptions to bring them into harmony with Morgan's scheme, came to represent Aztec social organization in the image of the Iroquois. Mexicans and Peruvians had never advanced beyond a clan system, had retained as the basis of social relationships kinship ties rather than economic or territorial ones (White 1940:11–63).

Some Washingtonians. Paradoxical as it may sound, the most solid contributions came not from the colorful, impressive personalities just treated, but from several unpretentious workers. Who nowadays reads Brinton or Powell or McGee, whether for facts or ideas? But Jesse Walter Fewkes (1850–1930), Otis T. Mason (1838–1908), and Walter Hough (1859–1935) are still far from negligible in their respective fields of specialization.

Selected Writings

Fewkes started as a zoologist, as a one-time student of Louis Agassiz at Harvard, but later turned ethnographer and archeologist. When publishing on protozoa in his early days, he once told me, he found that only half a dozen people in the world would read his papers, so he shifted to anthropology. One cannot help wondering how large a public he acquired by his meticulously thorough, but soporific descriptions of Hopi ceremonial. The fact remains that the specialists have profited from them: Haeberlin cites thirty-two of Fewkes' papers in his doctoral dissertation, and fifteen were used by Elsie Clews Parsons in her work on *Pueblo Indian Religion*. What is more, Fewkes was an undisputed innovator in introducing sound-recording into field work (1889), first among the Passamaquoddy, soon after among the Pueblos; and according to an exacting critic, "few anthropologists since have made such thorough and judicious use of sound-recording equipment" (Rowe 1953:914). He did not shine as a theorist, to be sure, as witness his naïve faith in the historic value of clan migration legends (Fewkes 1900); at all events, one did not have to worry whether Fewkes was substituting the figments of his fancy for aboriginal thinking.

Mason's impress on technological researches is apparent from a glance at the comparative studies of Wissler, Spier, Birket-Smith, and Nordenskiöld. Above all, his *Aboriginal American Baskety* (Mason 1904) has remained a classic, unsupplanted after half a century's investigation. Theoretically, he was indeed capable of dreary evolutionistic patter (Mason 1908), but even concerning interpretation there is something to be said on the credit side. Evolutionist though he might be after the fashion of his period, he by no means shut his eyes to the claims of diffusion. In fact, we owe to him an eminently sound exposition of the logic of the diffusionist problem (Mason 1895a), adducing the detailed similarities between Amur and Columbia River canoes. At Chicago (1893) he was one of those who combated Brinton's intransigent parallelism.

Hough's museum studies, though on a lesser scale, are roughly comparable to Mason's. He, too, broke a lance for diffusion, tracing Northwest American plate armor to Japan (Hough 1895); though Laufer showed that the specific provenience suggested by Hough was untenable, he upheld the broader theory of some Asiatic source and

Robert H. Lowie

praised Hough's "intensely interesting and valuable study" (Laufer 1914:260 *et seq.*).

In native capacity William H. Holmes (1846–1933) belongs on a higher level than the three men just considered. This judgment is not due to any personal preference on my part, for whereas Hough and Fewkes were distinctly genial in their attitude to a younger man, I found Holmes stiff and condescending. But Boas—emphatically no friend of Holmes—correctly described him orally as "a very able man." Lacking the flamboyance of Cushing, the imposing personality of Powell, the quaint charm of Bandelier, he was distinctly their superior in sobriety of judgment. An artist by training and endowment, he had the scientific rather than the artistic temperament.

A prehistorian, Holmes claims consideration here only insofar as his inquiries bear on cultural theory. This applies especially to his discussion of primitive art. Like the German architect Gottfried Semper, who preceded him by some twenty years but was not concerned with aborigines, Holmes stressed the influence of technique: "Geometric ornament is the offspring of technique" (Holmes 1886c: 465). "The more closely the ceramic art of the ancient peoples is studied the more decidedly it appears that it was profoundly influenced by the textile arts, and especially by basketry" (1886a:359). But elsewhere there is complementary attention to the effect of life forms. In the evolutionary era of anthropology it was normal to look for ultimate origins, and Holmes traced the rise of ceramic forms to the imitation of "natural originals," such as gourds, coconut shells, and bladders. Further, "unconscious embellishment" would result if the artificer imitated, say, the spines or ribs of mollusk shells; at a later stage "these features would be retained and copied for the pleasure they afforded" (1886c:446, 454). Though placing the "realistic pictorial stage" later than the appearance of "non-ideographic" elements, Holmes did not ignore them and states that their significance tends to be lost, so that they "are subsequently treated as purely decorative elements" (1886c:453–57). How this view can be made to harmonize with the dictum that geometric ornament is the offspring of technique is not easily understood. At all events, Holmes considered various possibilities in the course of his studies. What is more, he must be credited with anticipating, though perhaps not adequately elaborating, certain views associated with Boas. He mentions, in passing, the virtuoso's urge to play with his technique; and he clearly recognizes the tendency to read meaning into primarily nonsignificant designs (1886c:452; 1906:186).

At least one of Holmes' archeological conclusions bears on a basic ethnological issue. He proved decisively that the rude American artifacts suggesting European paleoliths were not to be regarded as their chronological equivalents. They did not indicate a stage of inferior craftsmanship, but individual miscarriage in the process of manufacturing a tool of superior ("neolithic") grade. Thus, morphological similarity could arise independently by "convergence," though Holmes did not so phrase his inference (Holmes 1919:75, 159 *et seq.*).

I have heard Holmes described as morbidly cautious, but do not find him so. We have seen that he did not simply brush aside McGee's Pleistocene find; and when confronted with marked coincidences in detailed features he was willing to accept some sort of "ethnic relationships" even if it meant linking an Alaskan wood carving with a clay replica from a grave in the Middle Mississippi valley (1886c:451).

So far, then, as the interpretation of facts was concerned, the scholars discussed in this section relied on evolution tempered with diffusion, against which latter only Cushing and Brinton took a determined stand. In any case, not one of them approached the stature of Morgan or Tylor, and certainly none of them advanced beyond these predecessors theoretically. When they turned to generalities, they were likely to fall into empty schematizing. It was when Cushing duplicated aboriginal implements, when Mason analyzed basketry weaves, and Hough demonstrated how rapidly fire could be produced with a simple palm-drill, that they added to our insight, showing what early invention implied and "how much original human thought has been bestowed" on perfecting them (Mason 1895b:229). But estimable as is Mason's essay on parallelism versus transmission, it hardly compares with Tylor's papers on the patolli game and on correlations (Tylor 1878, 1889). Nor does Mason's magnum opus attain the originality and thought value of Morgan's *Systems* (Morgan 1871), notwithstanding its obvious faults. Certainly none but Brinton among the group concerned himself, as Tylor and Morgan did, with most departments of culture on a global scale; and Brinton alas! did not advance any subdivision of anthropology.

II

Diffusion and Evolution, then, constituted the theoretical legacy acquired by the nascent anthropologists about the turn of the century. But these guiding principles came to be qualified, transmuted, and supplemented by the advent of ideas stemming from various extraneous sources. I shall consider the respective influences of geography, biology, history, psychology, and philosophy.

The impact of geography is perhaps most obvious. I am not referring to the theory of environmentalism as reflected in, say, Cushing's speculations on Pueblo origins, for against that aberration the younger generation was adequately inoculated. I have in mind rather the positive advance in distributional investigations.

Such problems had indeed obtruded themselves before. When obsidian tools turned up in an Ohio mound at least a thousand miles east of any possible source of supply, transmission was the only possible explanation (Holmes 1914:427, 430). Sporadically, as in Mason's treatment of the canoes from the Amur River, the intermittent occurrence of highly detailed similarities was solved in corresponding terms. Apart from such specific questions, curators faced the task of installing museum collections and devised arrangements based on geographical proximity. These efforts naturally culminated in the definition of culture areas (Holmes 1914).

What distinguished the new era was the *systematic* determination of distributions for purposes of historical interpretation. A geographer by training, Boas early (1895) applied the method to the study of Northwest Coast mythology (Boas 1940:425–36), thereby setting a pattern widely followed. It was, of course, a natural procedure for anyone geographically oriented, as witness Gudmund Hatt's disserta-

Selected Writings

tion on Arctic skin clothing (Hatt 1914). Further, it could be extended to so apparently elusive a phenomenon as the vision quest (Benedict 1922). What is more, whole cultures could be compared for major historical reconstructions. The avowed objective of the Jesup Expedition was the "precise determination of the geographical distribution of ideas and cultural forces" (Boas 1909:7). The extensive studies by Clark Wissler and Leslie Spier, paralleled by those of Erland Nordenskiöld and Kaj Birket-Smith abroad, may be mentioned as examples of distributional researches envisaging historical objectives.

Insofar as distributional researches tended to establish diffusion, they could not help affecting the theory of unilinear evolution. If the use of obsidian tools by Ohio mound-builders was impossible except through transmission from an outside source; if Columbia River Indians had got their canoes from the Amur; if Pueblo pottery was a consequence of Mexican stimuli, then these particular features in the respective cultures were not due to any laws of internal development. As unexceptionable instances of dissemination multiplied, the conviction gained ground that if such laws existed they were perhaps obscured to such an extent as to become unknowable. We are not at the moment concerned with the correctness of the inference, but with the historical fact that it was drawn.

III

It is a commonplace that the belief in cultural evolution is independent of Darwinism. Not to cite aboriginal myths, the idea was propounded by ancient Greek and Chinese philosophers. Bachofen's *Das Mutterrecht* (1861) appeared after *Origin of Species*, but the conservative Swiss jurist remained untouched by the scientific currents of his age. In fact, we know that he expounded his basic position at a philologists' congress as early as 1856 (Meuli 1948:1045).

However, it was Darwin's theories that stirred the intellectuals of the world, and among them the ethnologists. Darwin assumed progressive development insofar as descent of a more complex from a simpler form may be called "progress." This feature is indeed eliminated from Radcliffe-Brown's definition of *social* evolution

(Radcliffe-Brown 1947), but it pervaded the writings of the *cultural* evolutionists. In analogy to the biological philosophy of the times, Tylor recognized "stages of development or culture, each the outcome of previous history" and sought "to work out as systematically as possible a scheme of evolution." Notwithstanding occasional relapses in culture, he argued, the general course was upward (Tylor [1871] 1889:1, 20 f. 32, 62 ff.). The insistence on advancement is equally pronounced in Lewis H. Morgan and Powell, over-obtrusive in O. T. Mason's lists of change "from stone hammer to steam hammer," "from conch shell and rattle to orchestra," "from tribal deity to the Infinite and Omnipresent" (Mason 1908:187 *et seq.*).

Since the ethnological theories leaned on biology, a radical shift in biological views inevitably had repercussions in the sphere of cultural anthropology. Such a shift was indeed a reality by 1904.

Not that skeptics had been lacking before; in fact, they included some of the greatest figures of nineteenth century science—Richard Owen, Rudolf Virchow, Karl Ernst von Baer. But about the turn of the century doubt and discontent came to a head, not as the result of a religious crusade, but of the rise of experimental methods. Jacques Loeb, bent on reducing the phenomena of life to the physics and chemistry of matter, was at one with the neovitalist Hans Driesch in looking with a mixture of pity and disdain on the "speculative and descriptive orientation" of the phylogenists.

A Columbia student who from a boy had accepted Darwinism as a dogma, who had steeped himself as an undergraduate in Herbert Spencer's *First Principles* and hailed Ernst Haeckel's *Die Welträtsel* as a definitive solution of all cosmic enigmas, was profoundly disturbed when browsing in the departmental libraries of Schermerhorn Hall or talking to age-mates who majored in zoology. Bewildering judgments turned up in the new books and journals. Haeckel, it seemed, was an irresponsible hotspur, if not a forger of evidence. For William James, Herbert Spencer was a "vague writer," and in Pearson's opinion the British philosopher cut a sorry figure when using the terms of physics. Darwin himself, esteemed for his monographs, was not always taken seriously as a theorist. In the building where our student spent most of his time Thomas Hunt Morgan, a

Selected Writings

prophet of the new dispensation, held forth on the weaknesses of the Darwinian philosophy.

To mention some of Morgan's points, he cited Johannsen's experiments on the inefficacy of natural selection: in a pure line the selection of particular individuals for breeding had proved immaterial. As for the "biogenetic law," the embryonic resemblances of higher and lower forms admitted of a simpler, alternative explanation than Haeckel's view that ontogeny rapidly recapitulated phylogeny. The paleontological record, with all its deficiencies, was indeed admitted as evidence of evolution, but it could never reveal "the hereditary units which have made the process of evolution possible." Perhaps most disturbing of all was the critique of the Darwinian's argument from comparative anatomy. Certainly one could make a plausible showing of widely diverging types that were linked by graduated steps. But was this more than a logical arrangement of data, suggesting at best what *might* have happened? Experiments had shown that 125 true-breeding mutants could be produced from the wild fruit-fly, and one could then put them in a series, with normally winged forms at one end and wingless forms at the other. But one extreme had *not* been evolved from the other by many intermediate steps: the several mutants had developed independently of one another (T. H. Morgan 1916:7, 27, 159).

Comparative psychology gave aid and comfort to the skeptics. Before the laboratory experiments of Edward L. Thorndike the alleged proofs of links between animal and human mind shriveled into romanticizing, anecdotal trivialities.

It does not matter in this connection whether, or to what extent, the new attitude was warranted. The point is that by 1900 the intellectual climate had changed. The transports of delirious rapture were succeeded by the mood of the *Katzenjammer*. What had figured as the quintessence of scientific insight suddenly shrank into a farrago of dubious hypotheses. In short, sobriety reigned once more in professional circles. The revulsion of feeling was a piece with the nausea evoked among the German laboratory workers of the early nineteenth century by the excrescences of *Naturphilosophie*.

Cultural anthropology could not escape the empiricist trend, which was eloquently defined in the opening pages of the Reports of the Jesup Expedition:

"The history of anthropology is but a repetition of that of other sciences. . . . New facts are disclosed, and shake the foundations of theories that seemed firmly established. The beautiful, simple order is broken and the student stands aghast before the multitude and complexity of facts that belie the symmetry of the edifice that he had laboriously erected. Such was the history of geology, such the history of biology. . . . We are still searching for the laws that govern the growth of human culture, of human thought; but we recognize the fact that before we seek for what is common to all cultures, we must analyze each culture by careful and exact methods. . . ." (Boas 1898:3 f.).

Let us note that, as Thomas H. Morgan did not reject biological evolution in toto, neither did anthropologists reject all cultural evolution. As Morgan accepted the paleontological record, they accepted the testimony of prehistory. Beyond that they were willing to be convinced by evidence. Contrary to some misleading statements on the subject, there have been no responsible opponents of evolution as *scientifically proved,* though there has been determined hostility to an evolutionary metaphysics that falsifies the established facts. To adduce an a fortiori proof of this contention, Fathers Schmidt and Koppers (1924:382, 396 *et seq.,* 625 *et seq.,* 636) consistently speak of "development" (*Entwicklung*), "stages of the total development," "the step from lower to higher hunting," and so forth. They, like their independent associate Heine-Geldern (1937; 1955:7), welcome the teachings of prehistory; nothing is farther from their minds than a relapse into the degeneration theory combatted by Tylor in 1871. Like other critical culture-historians, they repudiate *unilinear* evolution while making due allowance in principle for internal development. To quote Father Schmidt (1937:111, 10): "I neither avoid the word nor the concept and fact of evolution, but . . . freely profess *evolution,* while now, as before, deprecating *evolutionism*" . . . ". . . He who combats and rejects evolutionism, is not thereby combatting and repudiating evolution, internal development."

Whoever wishes to understand the psychology of what has been inaccurately caled "the reactionary philosophy of anti-evolutionism" in anthropology would do well to ponder the attitude of Jacques Loeb, T. H. Morgan, and H. Driesch toward phylogenetic speculations. Critical votaries of both sciences had simply arrived at higher standards of proof.

IV

In the meantime, skepticism concerning evolutionary "laws" was also being fostered by philosophers and historians.

The "Southwest German" school of philosophy drew a sharp line between "nomothetic" and "idiographic" branches of learning, i.e. those which sought to establish laws and those which aimed at comprehending phenomena in their totality. Wilhelm Windelband formulated the antithesis in his rectoral address (1894), using for illustration physics and history (Windelband 1915). The essential distinction is doubtless older; it underlies an early paper of Boas' on the two approaches possible in geography (Boas [1887] 1940:626–47).

Windelband has been quoted by Radcliffe-Brown and myself, but his follower Heinrich Rickert seems to have made a deeper impression on ethnologists—possibly because he elaborated the issue at great length (Rickert 1899, 1896–1902). In Kroeber's collected essays there are eight references to him (Kroeber 1952:54, 70, 71, 73, 101, 123, 136, 469), and Sapir (1917:447) paid him a high compliment: "For a penetrating analysis of the fundamental distinction between historical and natural science I strongly urge all anthropologists, and social scientists generally, who are interested in method to refer to H. Rickert's difficult but masterly book on Die Grenzen der naturwissen-schaftlichen Begriffsbildung; eine Einleitung in die historischen Wissenschaften. I have been greatly indebted to it."

I surmise that Sapir's disinclination to put phonetic and natural "laws" on the same level stems from his indoctrination with Rickert's ideas. The reader of Windelband or Rickert might certainly conclude that the historical disciplines not only failed to demonstrate laws, but most emphatically did not wish to find any.

Robert H. Lowie

During the years under discussion historians themselves were clashing over the logic of their branch of knowledge, and their debates were echoed in our seminars. Indeed, two of the chief combatants, Karl Lamprecht and Eduard Meyer, lectured at Columbia. Lamprecht, scorning traditional historiography, insisted that it must be transformed into a true science, i.e. use the principle of causality as known to physicists and must determine laws. "Percepts" (*Anschauungen*) were to be superseded by "concepts" (*Begriffe*). Whole epochs could be subsumed under such concepts. Lamprecht had allegedly had some obtruded on him by a purely inductive study of the tenth and eleventh century in Germany. A "diapason" (a favorite term of his) penetrated all the psychic phenomena of a period, "all sentiments and actions." [Attention, Configurationists!] The eras thus revealed for Germany turned out to have correspondences in the past of other great nations; the psychic characteristics of periods succeeded one another in regular sequence and were causally linked (Lamprecht 1900:14, 16 ff., 25 ff., 33 ff.).

A colleague of Lamprecht's at Berlin deliberately carried the fight into the ethnological arena, dealing with Tungus and Papuans, Chukchi and Australians (Breysig 1904; 1936:433 ff.). He not only believed in fixed sequences, but also preached a return to Bastian and to a universal parallelism.

This new dispensation manifestly ran counter to Windelband's and Rickert's philosophy, which found a valiant champion in Eduard Meyer, the dean of German historians of antiquity. In agreement with Rickert, Meyer declared that throughout his long experience he had never encountered an historical law. History was indeed a science, but its distinctiveness as such lay precisely in dealing with unique phenomena. In devastating sentences Meyer exposed Lamprecht's reliance on empty catchwords, and exploded Breysig's "laws" as so much pretentious drivel. Positively, he defined history as the science which determined past facts, selecting from their infinite number those which had proved effective, *wirksam* (Meyer 1910:3–67). The issue seems perennial within the guild, as indicated by an eminent Dutch scholar's treatment of it a generation later (Huizinga 1943:24 f., 40, 42, 46, 52).

Selected Writings

Directly or indirectly, the idiographic conception of history affected incipient ethnologists. Thus, in 1909 a recent Ph.D. deprecated Schurtz's and Webster's "belief in a law of social evolution" as "unhistorical." Each tribal series of the age-societies he was studying must be investigated as "a unique historical product" (Lowie 1909: 75, 98).

Of course, neither Columbia nor America had a monopoly of such points of view. When Wilson D. Wallis returned to the United States from his Oxonian interlude, he made it clear that R. R. Marett had also turned from unilinear evolutionism and was preaching the need for regional specialization (Wallis 1912:178 *et seq.*).

V

The singularity of past events was not the only lesson to be learned from history. Evolutionists were mostly continuators of the tradition of French encyclopedism. The votaries of *éclaircissement* had gauged past epochs by the norms of Western Europe in the eighteenth century: earlier periods ranked higher or lower as they approached the assessors' own age, so that medieval times, in particular, received a very low grade indeed.

The investigators of culture in the second half of the last century had only in part emancipated themselves from such complacency. Lord Avebury (Sir John Lubbock) was constantly chagrined and shocked by the "disgusting" Hottentot, the "miserable" Australian, the "cruel" savages "almost entirely wanting in moral feeling" (Avebury 1872:430, 437, 448, 509, 511, 536, 576; 1911:414). Indeed, the evolutionists of the period by no means spared those Western civilizations which happened to deviate from their own. L. H. Morgan's diaries while traveling in Europe illuminatingly exhibit this parochialism. The Italians, he averred, were "degraded beyond all other peoples called civilized," the South Italians were "utterly worthless." On the other hand, the United States ranked as "the favored and the blessed land. Our institutions are unrivaled and our people the most advanced in intelligence" (White ed. 1937:285, 290, 303, 311, 315, 327).

Yet as early as 1774 Herder had proclaimed in unmistakable terms that every people and each period in its past should be judged not by extraneous norms, but in accordance with local and temporal circumstances. The ancient Egyptian was not to be compared with the Hellene or with the eighteenth-century *philosophe*. In short, Herder championed what we now call "cultural relativism," and thereby he deeply influenced Western historiography (Herder, 1935: 153–190. Cf. Clark 1955:187 *et seq.*). James Harvey Robinson, who fifty years ago was lecturing to large audiences at Columbia on the history of the West European intellectual class, was in his general outlook very far to the left of center, but historical-mindedness was one of his cardinal principles and nothing could be more sympathetic than his account of St. Francis of Assisi. Incidentally, it was Robinson's lectures that fired Radin with the idea of studying the role and the attitude of the intellectual class among primitive peoples (Radin 1927:XII).

Herder was referred to in my first seminar and figures here and there in our teacher's writings. Whether Boas derived relevant principles from the German classic directly or indirectly, I do not know, but he unremittingly preached the necessity of seeing the native from within. As for moral judgments of aboriginal custom, we soon learnt to regard them as a display of anachronistic naïveté.

History presented ethnologists with more technical suggestions. Paul Radin had majored in history under Robinson before turning to anthropology for his life work. It is probably no accident that, uncongenial as Radin found Boas, he became his most scrupulous follower in the collection of raw documentary material (Robinson 1912; Radin 1933).

VI

Psychological science is still unable to answer some questions which an anthropologist would like to have illuminated for him. But between, say, 1900 and 1915 psychology had clarified several important problems—the relative inborn endowment of the races, the question of individual variability, the mental processes of primitive as compared with civilized man. On some of these questions, to be sure, aid came from outside the circle of professional psychologists.

Selected Writings

As early as 1858 Theodor Waitz had judiciously warned against underestimating the innate capacity of unlettered races, but it remained to probe the matter with the help of up-to-date techniques. In 1898 trained psychologists for the first time "investigated by means of adequate laboratory equipment a people in a low stage of culture under their ordinary conditions of life" (Haddon n.d.:62). The statement refers to W. H. R. Rivers' and his associates' studies among the Torres Straits Islanders, which he summarized some years later (Rivers 1901); the findings were reported on in one of James McKeen Cattell's seminars. At the St. Louis Fair (1904) Cattell's associate, Robert S. Woodworth (1910:171–86), investigated various ethnic groups and arrived at results comparable to those of the British researchers. Contrary to certain interpretations, these two independent investigations did not demonstrate identity of racial endowment, but they failed to discover radical differences and did not exclude environmental explanations of such differences as turned up. In other words, pending subsequent correction of these results, the ethnologist felt warranted in ignoring hypothetical differences; and with assurance he could reject the gospel of Gobineau and his followers.

It was otherwise with innate *individual* variability, a phenomenon forcibly brought home by Francis Galton, whose *Inquiries into Human Faculty and Its Development* (1883), according to Wm. James, marked a new era in the history of psychology. The book gave me one of the lamentably few thrills experienced in the course of much professional reading. The environment was indeed favorable to an appreciation of Galton. Cattell, who had worked with him in London, regarded him and James as the two most remarkable men he had known. Boas, I think, had at least met Galton and held him in high esteem. The application of Galton's principle to our field was inevitable. With it collapsed the dogma that aborigines were wholly submerged in their social setting; at the same time new lines of observation obtruded themselves. Ethnographers consciously noted the role of leaders, skeptics, and other deviants; they distinguished between esoteric and exoteric rituals and myths; they made it their business to record several versions of the same tale, to take heed of the individual craftsman's attitude toward his art. The entire problem of the individual's relation to his society loomed as one of major consequence—for English-trained Wallis no less than for the Columbia group (Wallis 1915:647 et seq.).

This new orientation corrected the sociological aversion to dealing with everything biographical and individual, as defined in Durkheim's Preface to his first Année (1898:VI). It also ran counter to Wundt's notion that on the primitive level the individual was negligible, Völkerpsychologie terminating precisely at the point where "history" began with individuals influencing further developments (Haeberlin 1916:279).

However, American anthropology, far from spurning the lessons of sociology, incorporated them into its stock of ideas. The individual mind certainly was not a blank tablet, as was so commonly assumed in plausible hypotheses of cultural origins. If Japanese carpenters use planes in one way and Western carpenters in another; if different Crow Indians repeatedly experience the same kind of visions while Ojibwa regularly see different things on their fasts, such psychological phenomena can be neither typical of the human species as a whole nor of single individuals, but of cultures. However important may be the individual's psyche, his psychological manifestations are at least co-determined by social standards.

How far back in European thought this realization can be traced, I do not know, but it is already crystal clear in Marx's and Engels' (1888) critique of Ludwig Feuerbach. That philosopher had reduced "the essence of religion to human nature. But human nature (*Wesen*) is not an abstract something inherent in the single individual. As a reality it is the ensemble of social relationships." The religious sentiment, the Socialist thinkers contended, is a social product; the individual analyzed by Feuerbach belonged to a definite social form (Engels 1946:55 f.).

From another starting-point Moritz Lazarus and Heymann Steinthal postulated a folk-soul, a notion already adumbrated by Herder, and developed it in the *Zeitschrift für Völkerpsychologie und Sprachwissenschaft* (1859). That journal, too, figured in a seminar I attended; and it is interesting to learn that Adolf Bastian, Boas' senior at the Berlin Museum, had been personally inspired by

Selected Writings

Lazarus (Schmidt and Koppers 1924:28). The notion of the folk-soul was further elaborated by Wundt, who recognized psychic manifestations "not to be explained solely by the characteristics of individual consciousness because they presuppose the interaction of many" (Wundt 1913:3).

If the individual's mental life was largely influenced by his society, this fact by itself implied that his thinking could be only in moderate degree rational. With or without a sociological orientation, a variety of authors kept harping on human irrationality. Gabriel Tarde's *Les lois de l'imitation* (1890) brought home to Boas the force of unconscious imitation and prestige suggestion (Boas 1940 [1896]:382). An economic geographer, Eduard Hahn, showed convincingly that sundry features of economic life could not possibly have originated in logical ratiocination (Hahn 1896, 1909, 1919). His main points were absorbed by Boas and Laufer, who passed them on to the younger generation. Laufer, independently of Hahn, strongly felt that the course of history was nonrational, and hence resistant to any logical scheme: "The unexpected, the unforeseen has always happened, and this is what cannot be supplied or supplemented by the logic of our rational mind" (Laufer 1914:261). Lévy-Bruhl (1910) went so far as to ascribe to primitive, as contrasted with civilized, man a prelogical mentality. The distinction was generally rejected, finally by its author himself, but the argument did convincingly support other evidence against picturing primitive man as formally solving his problems. Again, Wundt's psychology, even apart from his *Völkerpsychologie*, was definitely anti-intellectualistic. Finally may be mentioned the growing conviction among students of religion that ceremonial tended to precede the myth sanctioning it; in other words, behavior preceded thought.

The general import of all these views was to modify to a considerable degree the outline of religious development so impressively elaborated by Tylor. The great British anthropologist had represented early man as excogitating a veritable system of beliefs in answering the problems of human existence. Later scholars regarded relevant ideas as of unconscious growth, logical interpretation setting in only secondarily (Boas 1940:596). Marett presented the case in almost identical terms: The "fairly conscious inferences" ascribed to primitive man by Tylor must have been "preceded by an unconscious attitude of spontaneous behavior" (Wallis 1919:292).

Wundt's name has turned up several times in my discussion, and in view of his having devoted eleven volumes to *Völkerpsychologie* he can hardly be ignored. He was demonstrably read to some extent by Boas, Kroeber, Goldenweiser, Reichard, Haeberlin, and Lowie; from a conversation with Sapir I recall that he had at least read at Wundt, but was repelled by his diffuseness. Goldenweiser, on the other hand, on whom anything voluminously systematic cast a spell, put a very high value on Wundt's contribution to social science and dedicated a book to him (Goldenweiser 1933:189–98). He is obliged to admit Wundt's relapses into a superannuated evolutionism, but lavishes praise on his nonintellectualistic approach to the origin of early inventions. However, a scholar interested in culture history could have derived the same insights more naturally from Hahn and Laufer.

Nevertheless, I should not like to minimize Wundt's influence on ethnology, but think that his general psychological position proved more fruitful than his specific treatment of cultural data. Haeberlin was a student of Wundt's in Leipzig and has left us in incisive, though not unappreciative, critique of his former teacher's principles (Haeberlin 1916b:279–302). Although Haeberlin also attended Lamprecht's lectures and may have been stimulated by one aspect of the historian's thinking, I believe that the psychologist's influence was deeper. When Haeberlin formulated the concept of configuration, though not using the word (1916a:1–55), he was probably extending his master's concept of "the creative synthesis" of psychic action with its corollary of the totality transcending the sum of its elements (Wundt 1911:1–113; 1920:152–62).

VII

The period here dealt with was one of intellectual ferment far transcending the range of particular disciplines. The second, enlarged edition of Karl Pearson's *The Grammar of Science* and the second,

Selected Writings

enlarged edition of Ernst Mach's *Die Analyse der Empfindungen* appeared in 1900; H. Poincaré's *La science et l'hypothese* in 1903; Wilhelm Ostwald's *Vorlesungen über Naturphilosophie* in 1902. Crystallizing his earlier thoughts, Wm. James published *Pragmatism* in 1907, *A Pluralistic Universe* in 1909. John Dewey's instrumentalism was correctly felt to represent a related point of view. As Pearson remarked at the time, "many minds are being stirred to reconsider the fundamental concepts of science."

Students in eastern universities were not divorced from these currents. Dewey joined the Columbia faculty in 1904 and once, though much later, offered a joint seminar with Boas on comparative ethics. James and Ostwald lectured at Columbia in my day, and I recall an intimate conversation with Ostwald after he had addressed a seminar of Cattell's. Several of us, including Paul Radin, Goldenweiser, and myself, founded an informal "Pearson Circle" for the discussion of *The Grammar of Science* and continued our meetings long after we had left the University. The group naturally included nonanthropologists, among them the philosopher Morris R. Cohen, to whom S. F. Nadel has acknowledged his indebtedness.

What has all this to do with anthropology? Simply this: the anthropology of fifty years ago was not the concoction of "isolationists" (as they have been branded by some younger colleagues). We were not wholly concerned with finding out whether the Plains Indians put up tipis on a foundation of three or of four poles. In philosophical terms, the ethnologists of that era had passed from a naïvely metaphysical to an epistemological stage and in this were reflecting the spirit of the times. . . .

What impressed me in those days was that in a sense Meyer, Boas, and Mach were doing much the same thing. They were severally scrutinizing such blanket terms as "schizophrenia," "totemism," "matter" and trying to discover their factual basis. When I grappled with Schurtz's notion of "age-society" and later with L. H. Morgan's of "classificatory terms of relationship," I more or less consciously applied the principles of these scientific thinkers. We had learned to view catchwords with suspicion.

Robert H. Lowie

In the present article I have not tried to write a history of intellectual movements; I have merely drawn attention to those currents of thought which certainly or at least probably bore on the history of American anthropology.

BIBLIOGRAPHY

Avebury, Lord (Lubbock, Sir John)
    1911 [1872]   The origin of civilisation and the primitive condition of man. London.

Bandelier, Adolphe
    1877   On the art of war and mode of warfare of the ancient Mexicans. Tenth Report, Peabody Museum:95–161.
    1878   On the tenure and distribution of lands, and the customs with respect to inheritance, among the ancient Mexicans. Eleventh Report, same series:385–448.
    1879   On the social organization and mode of descent of the ancient Mexicans. Twelfth Report, same series:557–669.

Benedict, Ruth Fulton
    1922   The vision in Plains culture. American Anthropologist 24:1–23.

Boas, Franz
    1898   The Jesup North Pacific expedition. Introduction. American Museum of Natural History, Memoir 2:3–6.
    1896   Die Entwicklung der Geheimbünde der Kwakiutl-Indianer. Festschrift für Adolf Bastian.
    1909   Die Resultate der Jesup Expedition. International Congress of Americanists XVI:1–18. Vienna, Separat-Abdruck.
    1940   Race, language and culture. New York.

Breysig, Kurt
    1904   Der Stufenbau und die Gesetze der Weltgeschichte.
    1936   Die Geschichte der Menschheit I: Die Anfänge der Menschheit. Breslau.

Brinton, Daniel Garrison
    1868   The myths of the New World. Philadelphia.
    1891   The American race. New York.
    1898   Religions of primitive peoples.
    1901   Races and peoples; lectures on the science of ethnography.

Bunzel, Ruth
    1932   Zuñi origin myths. Bureau of American Ethnology, Annual Reports 47:545–609.

Clark, Robert T. Jr.
    1955   Herder. Berkeley.

Cushing, Frank Hamilton
    1886   A study of Pueblo pottery as illustrative of Zuñi culture. Bureau of American Ethnology, Report 4:473–521.
    1891   Outline of Zuñi creation myths. Bureau of American Ethnology, Report 13.

1920 [originally 1884–85] Zuñi breadstuff. Indian Notes and Monographs, vol. VIII. New York.

Durkheim, Emile
1898 L'année sociologique I. Paris.

Engels, Friedrich
1946 Ludwig Feuerbach und der Ausgang der Klassischen deutschen Philosophie. Berlin.

Fewkes, Jesse Walter
1900 Tusayan migration traditions. Bureau of American Ethnology, Annual Report:19.

Goldenweiser, A. A.
1933 History, psychology, and culture. New York.

Haberlin, Herman K.
1916a The idea of fertilization in the culture of the Pueblo Indians. American Anthropological Association, Memoir 3.
1916b The theoretical foundations of Wundt's folk psychology. Psychological Review 23:279–302.

Haddon, Alfred C.
n.d. History of anthropology. London.

Hahn, Eduard
1896 Die Haustiere und ihre Beziehungen zur Wirtschaft. Leipzig.
1905 Das Alter der wirtschaftlichen Kultur. Heidelberg.
1919 Von der Hacke zum Pflug. Leipzig.

Hatt, Gudmund
1914 Arktiske Skinddragter i Eurasien og Amerika. Copenhagen.

Heine-Geldern, Robert
1937 L'art pre-Bouddique de la Chine et de l'Asie du Sud-est et son influence en Océanie. Revue des Arts Asiatiques, XI, fascicule 4:177–206.
1955 Die Zukunft der Völkerkunde. Kontinente, May 1955:5–9.

Herder, Johann Gotfried
1935 [1774] Auch eine Philosophie der Geschichte zur Bildung der Menschheit. (*in* Koch, Willi, ed., Herder, Mensch und Geschichte. Leipzig.)

Hodge, F. W.
1912 Obituary of W. J. McGee. American Anthropologist 14:683–687.

Holmes, William H.
1886a Pottery of the ancient Pueblos. Bureau of American Ethnology Reports 4:257–360.
1886b Ancient pottery of the Mississippi Valley. Same volume:361–436.
1886c Origin and development of form and ornament in ceramic art. Same volume:437–465.
1893 The World's Fair Congress of Anthropology. American Anthropologist. o.s. 6:423–434.
1906 Decorative art of the aborigines of North America. Boas Anniversary Volume:179–188. New York.

Robert H. Lowie
- 1914   Areas of American culture characterization. American Anthropologist 16:413–446.
- 1919   Handbook of aboriginal American antiquities I. Bureau of American Ethnology, Bulletin 60.

Hough, Walter
- 1892   The methods of fire-making. U. S. National Museum Report for 1890.
- 1895   Primitive American armor. Same series, Report for 1893:625–651.

Huizinga, J.
- 1943   Im Bann der Geschichte. Basel.

Kroeber, A. L.
- 1931   The Seri. Southwest Museum Papers, No. 6. Los Angeles.
- 1952   The nature of culture. Chicago.

Lamprecht, Karl
- 1900   Die kulturhistorische Methode. Berlin.

Laufer, Berthold
- 1914   Chinese clay figures I. Field Museum Anthropological Series 13:73–315.

Lévy-Bruhl, Lucien
- 1910   Les fonctions sociales dans les sociétés inférieures. Paris.

Lowie, Robert H.
- 1909   The Assiniboine. American Museum of Natural History, Anthropological Papers 4:1–270.

Mason, Otis T.
- 1895a   Similarities in culture. American Anthropologist. o.s. 8:101–117.
- 1895b   The origins of invention. London.
- 1904   Aboriginal American basketry. U.S. National Museum, Report for 1902:171–548.
- 1908   Mind and matter in culture. American Anthropologist 10:187–196.

Meyer, Eduard
- 1910   Kleine Schriften. Berlin.

McGee, W. J.
- 1898   The Seri Indians. Bureau of American Ethnology Annual Reports 17, pt. 1:1–344.
- 1955   An obsidian implement from Pleistocene deposits in Nevada. [American Anthropologist o.s. 2:Oct. 1st, 1889.] Reprinted in Reports of the University of California Archaeological Survey, No. 32:30–38.

Meuli, Karl
- 1948   Nachwort in Bachofen, Johann Jakob, Das Mutterrecht:1011–1128. Basel.

Morgan, Lewis H.
- 1871   Systems of consanguinity and affinity. Washington.
- 1877   Ancient society. Chicago. [Kerr edition]

Morgan, Thomas Hunt
- 1916   A critique of the theory of evolution. Princeton.

Powell, John Wesley
- 1881   Sketch of the mythology of the North American Indians. Bureau of American Ethnology Reports 1:19–56.

Selected Writings

1888   From barbarism to civilization. American Anthropologist o.s. 1:97–123.
1891   Indian linguistic families. Bureau of American Ethnology Reports 7:1–142.
1896   On primitive institutions. Philadelphia.
1903   Report of the Director. Bureau of American Ethnology Reports 21:I–XL.

Radcliffe-Brown, A. R.
1923   The methods of ethnology and social anthropology. South African Journal of Science 20:124–147.
1947   Evolution, social or cultural? American Anthropologist 49:78–83.

Radin, Paul
1927   Primitive man as philosopher. New York.
1933   The method and theory of ethnology. New York.

Rickert, Heinrich
1896–1902   Die Grenzen der naturwissenschaftlichen Begriffsbildung; eine Einleitung in die historischen Wissenschaften. Tübingen, J. C. B. Mohr (P. Siebeck).
1926 [1899]   Kulturwissenschaft und Naturwissenschaft. Tübingen, J. C. B. Mohr (P. Siebeck).

Rivers, W. H. R. et al.
1901   Report of the Cambridge anthropological expedition to Torres Straits. Vol. II. Pt. I. Cambridge.

Robinson, James Henry
1912   The new history. New York.

Rowe, John Howland
1953   Technical aids in anthropology: a historical survey. *In* Anthropology Today. Chicago, University of Chicago Press.

Sapir, Edward
1917   Do we need a "superorganic"? American Anthropologist 19:414–447.

Schmidt, Wilhelm
1937   Handbuch der Methode der kulturhistorischen Ethnologie. Münster.

Schmidt, Wm. and Wm. Koppers
1924   Völker und Kulturen. Regensburg.

Smyth, Albert H. et al.
1900   Brinton memorial meeting, June 16th, 1900. Philadelphia, American Philosophical Society.

Tarde, Gabriel
1890   Les lois de l'imitation. Paris.

Tylor, Edward B.
1878   Researches into the early history of mankind and the development of civilization. London.
1889 [1871]   Primitive culture. New York. 2 vols.

Wallis, Wilson D.
1912   The methods of English ethnologists. American Anthropologist 14:178–186.
1915   Individual initiative and social compulsion. American Anthropologist 17:647–665.
1919   The animistic hypothesis. American Anthropologist 21:292–295.

Robert H. Lowie

White, Leslie, ed.
    1937   Extracts of Lewis H. Morgan's European travel journals. Rochester Historical Society Publications vol. XVI. Rochester.
    1940   Pioneers in American anthropology; the Bandelier-Morgan letters, 1873–1883. 2 vols. Albuquerque.

Windelband, Wilhelm
    1915   Präludien. Tübingen.

Woodworth, Robert S.
    1910   Address of the Vice President and Chairman of Section H of the American Association for the Advancement of Science, Boston, 1907. Science:171–186.

Wundt, Wilhelm
    1911   Kleine Schriften. Leipzig.
    1913   Elemente der Völkerpsychologie. Leipzig.
    1920   Völkerpsychologie X. Leipzig.

The following essay is the first of a series of four lectures —the first two of which were published—given at the American Museum of Natural History. "Social Organization" is of signal importance as Lowie's first systematic theoretical attack on the classical theory of unilinear evolutionism (see pages 44–71, above, for a discussion of the totality of this debate). The paper outlines his own theoretical position and should be regarded as a precursor of his book Primitive Society, *which appeared six years later. It reveals the keenness of Lowie's analytic approach, his gift for examining the diversity within what is believed to be unitary, and his method of sorting out all the variables in any institution and subjecting them to unsparing comparative scrutiny.*

Lewis Henry Morgan's view of clanship and the role of the clan in social evolution is the subject of Lowie's critique. In this first lecture, he marshals empirical evidence against Morgan's view that unilineal descent groups were universal to North American Indian society, showing that such systems were found mainly in certain geographically continuous regions: the eastern United States, the Southwest, the Pacific Northwest, and sporadically in the Plains. Lowie also found that unilineal descent was conspicuously absent in the least complex societies and present in the more developed horticultural groups. This is not only contrary to Morgan's views on the antiquity of the clan, but the observation has also served as the basis for most recent evolutionary theory on social organization, which has tended to see unilineal descent as emergent with greater complexity and increased population. Lowie's other aim in this article was to refute the notion that matrilineal descent groups, or clans, preceded patrilineal descent, or gens. His evidence indicated little proof for Morgan's hypothesis, and he concluded that the gens need not derive from the clan, but that either clan or gens could arise from a prior condition of bilaterality, or lack of any form of unilineal descent. This is a thesis with which almost all recent evolutionary theorists would agree. The article, then, is not only a fine example of Lowie's critical writing, but also elegant evidence that Lowie was laying the groundwork for a less fanciful and scientifically sounder theory of social evolution.

Social Organization *

I

✤ Like the generation of thinkers that preceded ours, we are living in an age of revolt, but the object of our revolt is different from theirs. Our predecessors fought tradition as arrayed against reason. We have the task of exorcising the ghosts of tradition raised in the name of reason herself. There is not only a folklore of popular belief, but also a folklore of philosophical and scientific system-mongers. Our present duty is to separate scientific fact from its envelope of scientific folklore. This duty has been recognized by workers in various fields. And so we have in philosophy James's protest against monistic mythology; in physics and chemistry Mach's protest against mechanistic mythology; in biology and anthropology a no less vigorous protest against evolutionary mythology. Monism, mechanism, evolution are doubtless valuable con-

---

* *American Journal of Sociology*, Vol. 20, pp. 68-97, 1914. Two lectures (in a course of four) delivered in January under the auspices of the Department of Anthropology, American Museum of Natural History.

cepts; but they are valuable in proportion as they are free from scientific folklore.

[This article] is designed to help in the separation of anthropological fact from anthropological folklore. This is the more necessary because not only laymen but even scientists of neighboring fields—historians, economists, sociologists, social reformers—continue to use as definitely established truths anthropological theories that are now gracing only the refuse heaps of the modern anthropologist's laboratory.

I will confine my attention to a single problem—that of the clan and the gens, or, to call both by a generic term, that of the one-sided exogamous kinship group, a group that traces descent either through the father or through the mother exclusively, and within which marriage is prohibited (exogamy). I will outline the conception of this group in older anthropological literature. I will show why we secessionists revolt against that conception. And I will attempt to show how nowadays we grapple with the range of facts that concept was intended to summarize.

The concept we are here concerned with has been most clearly defined by Lewis H. Morgan in his *Ancient Society*, a work that has molded the views of innumerable professional and nonprofessional students of anthropology on the social organization of primitive tribes. This is not the place to define accurately Morgan's place in the history of anthropology. To avoid misunderstanding, I will state at the outset that in my opinion that place will remain a high one. But we must distinguish between Morgan the observer, and Morgan the theorist; and in Morgan's theoretical work we must again distinguish between his unusual power to see the importance of certain facts that had escaped others, and the very ordinary power shown in his naïvely synthetic constructions. Morgan's observations have indeed been challenged in part, yet in almost every instance, not only with reference to the Iroquois but also as regards tribes he was less intimate with, they have been corroborated by later and more thorough investigation. We are, therefore, entitled to consider him a painstaking, trustworthy observer. On the other hand, Morgan's interpretation of human society as a whole was not only unduly colored by his personal observations among the Iroquois, but reflected the trend of his age toward artificial evolutionary schemes. To develop such a scheme requires more than average ability, but, contrary to current notions, it does not require a very high grade of ability, certainly not of *scientific* ability. This Morgan displayed in a far more convincing manner when he noted the character of the Iroquois kinship system as distinct from our own, defined it, and set about with truly Darwinian industry to determine its analogues the world over. This genuinely scientific and theoretically important undertaking was doubtless not so spectacular as the interpretative speculations he superadded to the facts, but it will be rated higher by future generations.

To attack our problem. In *Ancient Society* Morgan's general aim is to trace the history of social organization from the period of savagery to that of latter-day civilization. This development, he contends, took place through a series of unconscious reformatory movements enforced by natural selection. Low down in the scale of savagery there was a period of intermarriage of brothers and sisters in a group. At a later stage this was prevented by forming social units that would include brothers and sisters (as well as many other member of the tribe), and prohibiting marriage between all members of the new units. These organizations were of two distinct types according to whether kinship was traced through the mother or the father: they were either what are now known as "clans" or what we now call "gentes." A clan consists of "a supposed female ancestor and her children, together with the children of her female descendants, through females, in perpetuity." A gens consists of "a supposed male ancestor and his children, together with the children of his male descendants, through males, in perpetuity." Both the clan and the gens would bar intermarriage of brothers and sisters, and also marriage of cousins, no matter how distant, belonging to the same kinship group. On the other hand, marriage was not thereby prevented between all blood relatives. With female descent, for example, I should not be permitted to marry my mother's sister's daughters, because they belong to my own clan, but I might marry my father's sister's daughters, who would necessarily belong to another clan. Morgan believes that, once invented, the scheme of the one-sided exogamous kin group spread "over immense areas through the superior powers of an improved stock thus created." With the exception of Polynesia, it formed "the nearly universal plan of government of ancient society, Asiatic, European, African, American, and Australian."[1]

To this notion of the one-sided exogamous kin group Morgan added a theory of how that group developed from an archaic to a relatively modern form. In order to secure "the benefits of marrying out with unrelated persons," it would obviously be immaterial whether kinship is reckoned on the mother's or father's side, so long as an equal number of relatives were prevented from mating. But Morgan holds that at the time when the one-sided exogamous group originated "marriage between single pairs was unknown, and descent through males could not be traced with certainty" (p. 67). Hence, he contends, in the archaic form of the kin group, kinship could be reckoned only in the maternal line, which also determined inheritance. When the paternity of children was assured, Morgan assumes that fathers revolted at their children being disinherited by the clan rule of inheritance, and in this way descent in the female line was overthrown and patrilineal descent substituted: in modern terminology, the clan was changed into a gens. Such, at least, is Morgan's account for the change among the Greeks and Romans (p. 345). For the Indian tribes with gentes he does not venture to suggest throughout the same motive for the development of the gens from the clan. Speaking of the Siouan family, he writes: "It is surprising that so many tribes of this stock should have changed descent from the female line to the male, because when first known the idea of property was substantially undeveloped, or but slightly beyond the germinating stage, and could hardly, as among the Greeks and Romans, have been the operative cause. It is probable that it occurred at a recent period under American and missionary influences" (p. 157). In general it may fairly be said that Morgan regards descent traced through the father as a quite recent institu-

[1] *Ancient Society*, pp. 27, 63, 74, 377–79. I am using the term "gens" not in Morgan's sense, but in that now common among American ethnologists.

tion, and believes in the ancient universality of the clan among North American Indian tribes (e.g., p. 177).

It is my intention to test Morgan's theory by the Indian data on which it is primarily founded. We may begin our test with the two most tangible questions that develop in connection with Morgan's scheme. Was the one-sided exogamous kinship group really a universal institution among the natives of North America? And did the exogamous gentes found among them develop uniformly out of exogamous clans? These questions have been answered by Dr. Swanton,[2] in the light of modern investigation, and while still later research has corrected his statement of the case in detail I find myself in full agreement with his general conclusions.

In answering the first question it would not serve our purpose to enumerate the tribes that have exogamous kinship groups and set off against them the tribes that have not. For in this manner the real meaning of the facts would often be obscured through lack of weighting. For the question of the ancient universality of the exogamous kinship group it is not equally significant whether the institution occurs among two quite unrelated tribes or among two tribes which, like the Hidatsa and Crow or some of the Southern Siouan tribes, have only branched out from a common ancestral tribe during the last four or five centuries. And obviously the recent adoption of a clan or gentile system, which in a fair number of instances is demonstrably a result of borrowing from neighboring tribes, is of no importance from this particular point of view. Fortunately the essential facts can be expressed in a somewhat summary fashion, owing to the geographical continuity of the tribes possessing the system in question. We find it, roughly speaking, in the greater part of the United States, east of the Mississippi, and some of the adjoining Canadian territory; among the Caddo and Southern Siouan tribes of the Plains, as well as among several of the Northwestern peoples in the same area; in New Mexico and Arizona; on the coast of British Columbia and Alaska and in part of the Northwest coast hinterland. There are thus four fairly con-

[2] "The Social Organization of American Tribes," *American Anthropologist*, 1905, pp. 663–73.

tinuous areas within which the one-sided exogamous kin group is known to exist. In the remaining part of North America north of Mexico no such institution has been discovered. Among the Eskimo, throughout the Mackenzie River and Plateau areas, as well as in nearly all of California and several of the Plains tribes, diligent inquiry has failed to reveal any trace of such an exogamous system. It cannot be supposed that the system did exist in these regions but has escaped the notice of observers. For there is nothing esoteric about the rule that kin must not intermarry; and where exogamous groups occur the social activities connected with them are so prominent that, according to the experience of American field workers, their existence is very readily ascertained. The supporters of Morgan's views must, therefore, reckon with the fact that the supposedly universal organization simply does not exist in a very large part of North America. It might be asserted that the system had once existed everywhere, but that in certain districts it has disappeared. But this remains a baseless assertion in the absence of any proof that such a process has occurred and in the absence of any reason for such a process of degeneration in the regions concerned. It cannot be maintained either that the tribes in question have advanced beyond the clan or gentile stage. When we compare the culture of the Shoshone, Paiute, Thompson River Indians, and others lacking the one-sided exogamous kin group with the Pueblo Indians, Iroquois, Omaha, and others possessing the system, it is at once apparent that whether from the point of view of industrial arts, social life, or ceremonial activity the tribes possessing the system are the more advanced. Swanton has rightly emphasized the fact that almost all the tribes with a clan or gentile organization are agriculturists, while the rest are almost all non-agricultural. The weight of such considerations as these has led Frazer—in other ways a typical representative of the classical school in anthropology—to reject Morgan's position and to admit that the stage of the exogamous clan or gentile system had never been attained by "the more backward members of the Redskin family." [3]

[3] *Totemism and Exogamy*, III, 1–3.

This statement of the facts must not, however, be interpreted to mean that the tribes in question represent a stage preceding that of the clan in Morgan's scheme. For in that case we should expect no definite restriction of marriage, even between own brothers and sisters,[4] while on the contrary we almost uniformly do find additional restrictions based on consanguinity. To cite only a few random examples: Among the Central Eskimo, marriages of cousins, nephews and aunts, nieces and uncles are prohibited.[5] Cousins are forbidden to marry among the Thompson River Indians, and even second-cousin marriages are disapproved.[6] In the Nez Percé tribe there were no restrictions of marriage except in the case of relatives, but even second or third cousins were not allowed to marry.[7] In these cases, of course, a superadded one-sided exogamous kin system would not "secure the benefits of marrying out with unrelated persons," because these benefits are already secured by existing marriage restrictions based on bonds of consanguinity. Thus the tribes in question in no way fit into Morgan's scheme of social evolution. They are not more advanced than the tribes possessing exogamous kin groups, for their general culture is undoubtedly lower. But neither are they so low in their social customs as to require an exogamous kin system for the retrenching of consanguine marriages. If anything, we should have to say that in this particular point they are higher, that is, nearer to our own mode of conduct, than the tribes organized in exogamous kin groups as conceived by Morgan.[8] It might still be argued that tribes may advance very unequally in different departments of culture; that therefore the loosely organized peoples may have lagged behind in their economic and industrial life while forging ahead of the tribes with clans or gentes in their social usages; that therefore they did once possess clans or gentes but have passed beyond that stage.

---

[4] Except in so far as the Australian four-class system prevailed, which, however, did not prevent first-cousin marriage (*Ancient Society*, pp. 425, 503).
[5] Boas, "The Central Eskimo," *Sixth Annual Report, Bureau of Ethnology*, p. 579.
[6] Teit, *The Thompson Indians of British Columbia*, p. 325.
[7] Spinden, *The Nez Percé Indians*, p. 250.
[8] This conception of Morgan's will, however, prove to be erroneous.

Robert H. Lowie

The general principle on which such an argument would rest is sound, but its application is highly unconvincing in the present case. It would never be applied except to save the endangered hypothesis, involving as it does an appeal not to any observable facts, but to our ignorance of unobservable ones. Accordingly, we may dismiss it and sum up our conclusion to the effect that in North America exogamous kin groups, instead of being universal, were absent from a great many tribes, and that these for the most part possessed a less complex culture than those who had this institution.

Let us now turn to our second problem. Has the history of the one-sided exogamous group in North America been the origin and partial persistence of the archaic clan and its partial transformation into a gens? In other words, have all the gentes found among our Indians been preceded by a clan system? It will be best to consider first the mechanism by which Morgan conceives the change to have occurred and then the question of fact involved.

Roughly speaking, we find the gentile (as opposed to the clan) system among the Central Algonkin, Blackfoot, and Southern Siouan Indians. For the last-mentioned tribes Morgan suggests, as already noted, that the hypothetical change occurred under American and missionary influences. This suggestion, however, is anything but convincing. We know of a number of instances where civilization has introduced novel social arrangements among Indian tribes, but of none where it has produced Morgan's hypothetical development. Among the Crow, for example, the government has introduced a patrilineal rule of property inheritance, but the native rule of maternal descent continues to hold for clan names and affiliations. The Iroquois have adopted the system of passing on surnames given by whites from father to son, but the ancient matrilineal system remains in full force. The Crow have probably been subject to white influence for as long a period as the Southern Siouan tribes, and the Iroquois doubtless for a much longer period. It seems highly improbable that within the short period of something like a century contact with civilization should have caused a considerable number of tribes not merely to adopt the white way of reckoning descent in matters that would be of moment in their dealings with whites, but to be so thoroughly imbued with the point

Selected Writings

of view of the whites as to adopt the alien mode of tracing lineage in all parts of their social system. The Mandan, of whom not a dozen full-blood members survive at the time of writing, still reckon tribal affiliation according to the matrilineal scheme; children of Mandan mothers and Hidatsa fathers are Mandan; children of Hidatsa mothers are Hidatsa. Morgan's suggestion as to the cause of change of descent among Siouan tribes may therefore be dismissed as unsatisfactory.

With reference to the Algonkian Shawnee, Morgan makes a suggestion more in accord with his general scheme of development (p. 169). Instead of ascribing the change of descent to civilized influence, he is here inclined to assign an internal cause—the wish to enable a son to succeed his father as chief, and to enable children to inherit property from their father. But, repeating in essence the foregoing remarks, we must insist that both these questions— descent of office and descent of property—do not necessarily affect the fundamental matter of reckoning lineage. The Crow illustration cited above fits in here also, for it is manifestly a matter of indifference whether the rule of inheritance is changed from alien or indigenous causes. The question is whether a change in the rules of property inheritance from the maternal to the paternal line is itself a cause of changing clan affiliations into gentile affiliations; and there seems to be no evidence for this alleged causal connection.

This does not answer the question of fact whether, regardless of what causes may have operated, the gens is a development from the clan. Morgan's proof consists essentially in pointing out that while certain tribes have a gentile system other members of the same stock have clans. This is of course a two-edged argument that may with equal force be used to prove that clans developed from gentes. From the fact that Mandan, Hidatsa, and Crow reckon descent in the female line, Morgan argues that the Ponka, Omaha, Iowa, and Kaw formerly reckoned descent in the same way (pp. 155 ff.), all these tribes speaking Siouan languages. So, from the occurrence of female descent among the Delaware, Morgan infers "its ancient universality in this form in the Algonkian tribes" (p. 172). To be sure, this conclusion is supported by some additional data. The Delaware are declared to be "recognized by all

117

Algonkian tribes as one of the oldest of their lineage," though it is safe to say that many Algonkian tribes were blissfully ignorant of the very existence of the Delaware in Morgan's time. Morgan furnishes better evidence in citing cases of several Algonkian tribes with male descent where nevertheless the chief's office was passed, not from father to son, but from maternal uncle to sister's son (pp. 166, 170). However, these cases are very few, have not been corroborated by later inquiry, and admit of other explanations. For example, there may be special rules for the inheritance of certain offices distinct from those which otherwise hold. The coexistence of different rules of descent for different social groups is well established in various primitive tribes. Thus, in Uganda descent of clan membership was patrilineal for all except princes of royal blood, who were always reckoned of kin with their mother. Considering that even with the most favorable interpretation of the cases cited by Morgan we are still confronted with a considerable number of tribes with paternal descent and no trace of any other system, we must conclude that Morgan has not established his scheme of development inductively but deduced it from his a priori postulate of unknowable fatherhood in archaic times.

This brings us face to face with a most important theoretical problem. We have indeed shown that Morgan has not proved his case from the North American data; but he may nevertheless be right if others have established the general law that matrilineal descent precedes paternal descent. Extending our inquiry beyond the American data, we must admit that until recently most sociologists and anthropologists deduced this sequence from such postulates as the uncertainty of fatherhood among primitive conditions. Tylor's point of view was doubtless in large measure determined by such considerations, but he supports it on a more solid basis of fact than is usually the case, and accordingly it will be best to consider his reasoning in some detail. Advancing what he himself characterizes as a geological argument, he holds that

> the institutions of man are as distinctly stratified as the earth on which he lives. They succeed each other in series substantially uni-

form over the globe, independent of what seem the comparatvely superficial differences of race and language, but shaped by similar human nature acting through successively changed conditions in savage, barbaric, and civilized life.

Tylor groups primitive tribes under three headings, corresponding to successive cultural strata: those with a maternal system of descent, those in which both maternal and paternal rules of descent coexist, and those with a purely paternal descent. He then examines, with reference to their occurrence in these strata, certain social customs—notably the remarriage of widows and the "couvade." His treatment of the latter case will suffice to illustrate the method of reasoning followed. The couvade is the practice (found most conspicuously in some parts of South America) by which "the father, on the birth of his child, makes a ceremonial pretense of being the mother, being nursed and taken care of, and performing other rites, such as fasting and abstaining from certain kinds of food or occupation, lest the new-born should suffer thereby." Tylor finds not a single instance of this strange usage among purely maternal peoples. In the maternal-paternal condition there are not less than twenty cases, while in the paternal the number dwindles to eight. From this Tylor infers that the purely maternal stage is the earliest because there is no survival of the couvade from other stages as there is in paternal society.

Just as the forms of life, and even the actual fossils of the Carboniferous formation, may be traced on into the Permian, but Permian types and fossils are absent from the Carboniferous strata formed before they came into existence, so here widow-inheritance and couvade, which, if the maternal system had been later than the paternal, would have lasted on into it, prove by their absence the priority of the maternal.[9]

[9] "On a Method of Investigating the Development of Institutions, Applied to Laws of Marriage and Descent," *Journal of the Anthropological Institute*, XVIII (1889), 245–69.

In support of Tylor's theory, that matrilineal institutions precede patrilineal descent, concrete evidence of all kinds has been adduced. Among the most recent writers, Rivers has expressed the conviction that this sequence holds for Oceania.[10] On the other side, American ethnologists have appealed to the case of the Kwakiutl of British Columbia, where there is assumed to have taken place a change in the contrary direction. According to Professor Boas, the Kwakiutl, like the tribes of Oregon, Washington, and southern Vancouver Island, once lived in village communities with paternal descent. Owing to the influence of the more northern Pacific tribes, whose system is matrilineal, the Kwakiutl grafted the northern principle of descent on that of the south, with the result that certain privileges are inherited in the paternal line and a much larger number are obtained by marriage through an intricate method that insures maternal descent.[11] But although the Kwakiutl facts are very interesting, it is highly doubtful whether they have the theoretical significance ascribed to them. It is, in the first place, worth noting that they represent, in Tylor's terminology, not a maternal but a maternal-paternal stage. At best, therefore, they yield evidence of change from a purely paternal to a *mixed* condition. Secondly, maternal descent, so far as it prevails, seems to be restricted to the inheritance of property, while the reckoning of a child's affiliation seems to be indeterminate, as we have been more recently informed by Boas that a child is reckoned as belonging to both his father's and his mother's family. Thirdly, it is a matter of grave doubt whether the Kwakiutl units of which maternal-paternal descent may be predicated correspond to the type of unit to which Morgan, at all events, applies the sequence advocated by himself and Tylor. For Morgan is speaking al the time of *exogamous* units, whether clans or gentes, and among the Kwakiutl there seems to be no definite rule of exogamy but only a preference for marriage out of the group, and even this is

[10] "Survival in Sociology," *The Sociological Review* (1913), pp. 293–305.
[11] Boas, "The Social Organization and the Secret Societies of the Kwakiutl Indians," *Report of the United States National Museum* (1895), pp. 334–35.

Selected Writings

denied in a later statement.[12] Finally, the Kwakiutl conditions are so specialized that adherents of the Tylor-Morgan theory may well regard them as exceptional; and even if the change from paternal to maternal descent be admitted, it is possible to suppose a pristine stage of matrilineal reckoning preceding the patrilineal village communities.

For these reasons the Kwakiutl conditions do not seem to furnish a favorable test case. Nevertheless, they embody the principle that forms the most vital objection to the classical theory as to rules of descent. For the Kwakiutl have developed their system not solely through internal growth but through contact with other tribes. The far-reaching influence of such connection with neighboring tribes generally has been realized to an increasing degree by modern anthropologists, and it obviously interferes with the doctrine of parallelism advanced by Tylor. For, granting that on account of the similarity of human nature, human institutions *tend* to succeed one another "in series substantially uniform over the globe," the borrowing of institutions would in an indefinite number of cases produce an abnormal sequence. We cannot even assert that where the observed sequence corresponds to the theory the result is due to uniform causes producing parallel evolution. Among the Carrier and Babine Indians there is matrilineal descent. As the majority of the Northern Athapascans, of whom these tribes form part, have a loose organization, it may be safely assumed that the Carrier and Babine once shared this sociological characteristic, provided we can indicate the conditions that in their case produced a change. We thus seem to have an illustration of the evolution of a clan system from the "earlier and less organized and regulated condition" postulated by both Morgan and Tylor. But the conditions that produced the change were not so general as the psychological constitution shared by humanity, but lay in the geographical contiguity of the Northwest Coast Indians, whose social

---

[12] Boas, *Annual Archaeological Report*, Toronto, 1905, pp. 239–40; Goldenweiser, "Totemism, an Analytical Study," *Journal of American Folk-Lore*, XXIII (1910), 187, 213.

121

Robert H. Lowie

organization was simply copied by the tribes in question. Accurate information as to the actual process of cultural development has largely shattered the belief once held in the necessity of parallel evolution among unrelated tribes. Many ethnologists now hold that historical processes are unique in character, that every phase of human history is so complicated by individual traits that no laws of historical development can be framed. This view has so deeply affected modern anthropology that even in quarters peculiarly liable to classical influence a far more cautious formulation is now in vogue. It is no longer contended that every gentile system has superseded a clan system, but merely that *if* the rule of descent changes at all, it changes from matrilineal to patrilineal descent. Thus, N. W. Thomas writes:

> whereas evidences of the passage from female to male reckoning may be observed, there is virtually none of a change in the opposite direction. In other words, where kinship is reckoned in the female line, there is no ground for supposing that it was ever hereditary in any other way. On the other hand, where kinship is reckoned in the male line, it is frequently not only legitimate but necessary to conclude that it has succeeded a system of female kinship. But this clearly does not mean that female descent has in all cases preceding the reckoning of kinship through males. Patrilineal descent may have been directly evolved without the intermediate stage of reckoning through females.[13]

And expressing a still more acceptable view, Cunow writes:

> Die meisten der heutigen vaterrechtlichen Halbkulturvölker haben sicherlich einst, wie sich deutlich aus ihren Rechtsbräuchen und Verwandtschaftsbezeichnungen nachweisen lässt, das Mutterrecht gekannt; aber das besagt noch nicht, wie den Vertretern der zweiten von Müller-Lyer genannten Theorie eingeräumt werden muss, dass das Mutterrecht eine Institution ist, die sich bei allen

---

[13] Thomas, *Kinship Organizations and Group Marriage in Australia*, p. 15. Also cf. Marett, *Anthropology*, p. 169.

Selected Writings

Rassen und Völkern ohne Unterschied auf gewisser Entwicklungshöhe einstellt. Unter besonderen Umständen mag das Mutterrecht ganz gefehlt haben oder doch die Mutterrechtsperiode von relativ kurzer Zeitdauer gewesen sein.[14]

From this modern point of view there is thus no reason to suppose that the Blackfoot, Central Algonkian, and Southern Siouan tribes ever possessed a clan system preceding their present or recent gentile system. Their general cultural condition, whatever may be the value of such a comparison, does not show a higher stage than that of maternally organized tribes; of the latter, indeed, the Pueblo Indians are manifestly superior to any of the patrilineal tribes. Considering the modified form in which such sane students as Marett, Cunow, and Thomas now present the classical theory of father-right and mother-right, we may safely say that there is no reason why the patrilineal tribes of North America could not have developed their system directly from a loose organization without passing through the hypothetical intermediate stage. Summing up, therefore, our reply to the two questions set at the beginning, we may say:

1. It is as certain as anything can be from the nature of the case that the one-sided exogamous kin-group system, whether in the form of clans or gentes, was not universal among North American tribes.

2. It is entirely unproved that those Indian tribes possessing a gentile system previously had a clan system.

This is the shorter and less technical of the two articles which appeared in 1915 under this title; reference to the other may be found in the bibliography of the text under Lowie 1915a. The debate over "classificatory systems" is fully discussed on pages

---

[14] Cunow, *Zur Urgeschichte der Ehe und Familie*, pp. 38–39.

59–65 above, and consultation of the charts in Figs. 1 and 2 (p. 63) will clarify several of the points raised by Lowie.

Although Lowie writes that he has substantiated the theory of Edward B. Tylor and W. H. R. Rivers that exogamy is a significant factor in the molding of kin term systems that merge lineal relatives with collateral ones, he actually added an important factor to the theory. Whereas Rivers emphasized marriage as the principal determinant, on the grounds that certain marriage forms will cause a conjunction of otherwise separate genealogical positions, or kin types, Lowie found that kin groups were the more influential variable. This is a view that has prevailed in the study of kinship nomenclature, and Lowie's specific position on the Crow and Omaha kinship systems has remained unassailable. Methodologically, Lowie's essay shows the development of the use of careful comparative analysis in the search for social causality, and his juxtaposition of two tribes of the same linguistic family, the Crow and the Omaha, is a way of controlling both the historical and linguistic variables in comparative study. This is the procedure which has become known as "controlled comparison" and has been used with felicitous results by Fred Eggan, Alexander Spoehr, and others.

Exogamy and the Classificatory System of Relationship*

✣ Lewis H. Morgan, in his *Systems of Consanguinity and Affinity* (Washington, 1871), established the fact that in a large part of North America, in India, in Africa, and in Oceania the natives use terms of relationship that designate not individuals but groups of individuals, and accordingly he labeled these systems as "classificatory." Later E. B. Tylor and others advanced the view that the classificatory system and exogamy—the rule that a person must marry outside of his own social group (clan or gens)—were merely two aspects of a single institution: that, in other words, primitive man classed together individuals belonging to the same exogamous

* *Proceedings* of the National Academy of Sciences, Vol. 1, pp. 346–49, 1915. Reproduced by permission of the Academy.

Selected Writings

division and separated individuals of different divisions. Quite recently this view has been advocated by W. H. R. Rivers. In his *Kinship and Social Organisation* (London, 1914) he correlates the classificatory system with exogamy, our own system with the family in the narrower sense of the term, and the descriptive system of, say, the Nilotic Negroes (in which a few primary terms designate the basic relationships and serve by their combination to describe all other relatives) with the patriarchal or extended family. The correlation of the classificatory nomenclature with exogamy now requires empirical verification in the several areas of the globe, and the following is an attempt to make this test for North America.

Before undertaking this inquiry, however, the concept "classificatory" must be supplanted by one that more adequately represents the phenomenon under discussion. For any particular "classificatory" system is not molded by a single factor but by a series of factors, and these are developed in varying degree in different systems. Hence the test must be applied to that common element which, consciously or unconsciously, differentiated the primitive terminologies in question from those current among ourselves in the minds of investigators. An examination of Morgan's earliest expressions on the subject indicates that it was the merging of lineal and collateral relatives—the use of a single term, e.g., for mother and mother's sister, for father and father's brother—that impressed this pioneer investigator, and this is the feature that actually characterizes the classificatory systems of all the regions of the globe. Our query is thus reduced to this form: Is the confusion of collateral with lineal relatives a function of exogamy?

The first question is, of course, how the exogamous tribes compare with those "loosely organized," i.e., those lacking exogamous divisions. One of the principal exogamous areas of North America is found in the United States east of the Mississippi. Practically throughout this immense territory the custom of exogamy is associated with a terminology that fails to distinguish collateral and lineal relatives. Among the Northwest Coast tribes of Canada the same association holds, and this applies likewise to those of the Plains tribes that possess a clan or gentile organization. The one doubtful exogamous region is the Southwest, for which we have practically no data except from the Tewa, where the correlation does *not* hold. An inquiry into the as yet unknown systems of the Keresan, Hopi, and Zuñi pueblos is of the highest theoretical importance. When we turn to the loosely organized tribes we meet again with one exceptional region, that of the Mackenzie River, and several sporadic cases outside, where nonexogamous tribes are reported to possess a kinship terminology that is *ex hypothesi* to be expected together with exogamy. On the whole, however, the agreement with the Tylor-Rivers theory is highly satisfactory. The Eskimo, the Plateau Indians, the Californian tribes are loosely organized; and all of them tend to emphasize the distinction of such relatives as father and paternal uncle, mother and maternal aunt. It is important to note that these terminologies by no means resemble those of European languages. Among the Shoshonean tribes and the Kootenai, for example, relatives distinguished in English are classed together through the extensive use of reciprocal terms, members of a related pair addressing each other by a common term. But these systems are "classificatory" only in an etymological sense of the word, the basis of the classification being wholly distinct from that which molds the collateral-lineal terminology of the systems customarily designated as "classificatory."

Summing up, we may say that there is a very high degree of correlation between the practice of exogamy and the ranging in a single category of collateral and lineal kin. The aberrant cases are relatively few and some of them are readily intelligible as the result of cultural influences from neighboring tribes. It is, of course, possible that the correlation may ultimately turn out to have an unexpected meaning, for example, that the emphasis on exogamy is misplaced and should be on definite organizations of any kind, whether exogamous or not. Such an interpretation might perhaps eliminate some of the at present anomalous instances of nonexogamous tribes sharing the nomenclature of exogamous peoples. At all events, the North American data furnish strong evidence in support of the Tylor-Rivers theory.

That the classification of kin by certain tribes is a function of the exogamous grouping, may be demonstrated in more rigorous fashion. Within the Siouan family there are tribes with kinship systems that not only fail to distinguish between collateral and lineal relatives but also class together members of distinct generations, which is contrary to the usual form of "classificatory" nomenclature. Rivers has suggested exceptional forms of marriage to account for the exceptional mode of classification; as a matter of fact it may be shown that the apparent exceptions are merely the result of an unusually consistent application of the exogamous principle of grouping.

The following are the facts. The Crow and Hidatsa, Siouan tribes tracing descent through the mother, class the father's sister's son with the father; the father's sister's daughter, father's sister's daughter's daughter and all her female descendants through females with the father's sister. It is to be proved that these classifications are connected with the exogamous social grouping.

The facts in the case may be summed up by saying that a single term is applied to male members of the father's clan regardless of generation, and a single term to female members of the father's clan who belong to his own and all descending generations. If this objective statement also represents the psychological basis of the grouping, the terminology should be modified as soon as we pass outside the clan. We pass outside the clan when we take not the father's sister's daughter's daughter, but the father's sister's *son's* daughter, since with exogamy and maternal descent she cannot belong to the father's clan. And actually we find that among the Hidatsa and Crow this relative is no longer classed with the father's sister but with the sister, this latter relationship following from the fact that *her* father is classed with *my* father. But between the status of a father's sister's daughter's daughter and a father's sister's son's daughter there is no ascertainable difference except that of clan affiliation. Therefore the terminological classification is a function of the exogamous group, which was to be proved.

The same conclusion may be established by eliminating the hypothetical factor in another way. The Siouan family embraces a number of tribes with patrilineal descent, of which the Omaha are the best known. In such tribes the father's sister's descendants are no longer,

Robert H. Lowie

as among the Crow or Hidatsa, members of the father's exogamous group; and we find, as a matter of fact, that her son and daughter are classed not with her but with the sister's son and daughter. With paternal descent my father's sister is my group sister, and while the Omaha have a distinct term for the father's sister it seems that in some ways she is still regarded as a sister—both as regards her children and as regards her husband, who is classed with the brother-in-law. On the other hand, the mother's brother's son, mother's brother's son's son, and so forth, are all members of the same exogamous group if there is paternal descent, and the Omaha actually designate them by a single term. And again, as soon as we pass out of the exogamous group, the terminology varies: my mother's brother's *daughter's* son is my brother, not my mother's brother, since he no longer belongs to my mother's gens but is related to me solely through his mother, who is my "mother" because *she* does belong to my mother's gens.

In short, passing from tribes with matrilineal to tribes with patrilineal descent within the Siouan stock, we find precisely those differences that logically follow from the assumption that the exogamous group lies at the basis of kinship classification; and passing within a particular tribe from relatives within the same group to relatives of otherwise similar status outside the group we at once find a difference in nomenclature. Hence the exogamous factor must have been a real cause in molding the kinship terminology of at least some so-called classificatory systems.

The Origin of the State, Chapter IV of which follows, appeared in 1927, and continued and expanded the directions taken by Lowie in Primitive Society *(1920). Characteristic of Lowie's complete dismissal of systematic economic determinism in general and Marxism in particular, the works of Marx and Engels are not cited throughout the book, and greater attention is paid instead to the theories of Franz Oppenheimer, who found the germ of the state in conquest. In any case, Lowie's work deals less with the historical causes of the state—be they economic, demographic, or political—than with the external, cultural characteristics of states and hierarchical systems. In the perspective of the more than four decades since its publication, the book has not proven to be of great influence in comparative political theory, except insofar as it clarified a number of questions for further research. Such illumination was, however, always one of Lowie's fortes.*

Lowie addressed his special attention to the question of whether the growth of the state was always accompanied by a shift from kinship as the sole basis of political organization to the principle of territoriality, a question which we raised in the text of the book on pp. 65–71. He documented the existence of various forms of territorial association and responsibility in primitive, nonstate societies, speculating on their significance as possible harbingers of centralized, coercive government. Beyond this refutation of the views of Maine and Morgan, he proceeded to demonstrate the extent to which territoriality, co-residence, and general neighborliness underlay what are ordinarily interpreted as kinship bonds, foreshadowing much important work that was yet to be done on the relation of kinship to practical activity. Lowie thus moved away from the tendency of the time to see kinship as inextricably tied to genealogical, biological connections, as a reality in itself, to the view that it is always a social creation. Consanguinity does not establish social relations; rather, social relations are phrased in the language of consanguinity. This is an interpretation held by almost all social anthropologists today, and Lowie was among the first to state it.

The Territorial Tie *

✣ In 1861 Sir Henry Sumner Maine, the father of comparative jurisprudence, sharply separated two principles of uniting individuals for governmental purposes—the blood tie and the territorial tie. He further combined this conceptual distinction with an *historical* theory, to wit, that in less advanced or earlier societies "kinship in

* *The Origin of the State*, Chapter IV, "The Territorial Tie," pp. 51–73. Copyright 1927, 1954 (New York: Russell & Russell, 1962).

blood is the sole possible ground of community in political functions." No revolution, he argued, could be "so startling and so complete as the change which is accomplished when some other principle—such as that, for instance, of *local contiguity*—establishes itself for the first time as the basis of common political action." And, again, he writes: ". . . the idea that a number of persons should exercise political rights in common simply because they happened to live within the same topographical limits was utterly strange and monstrous to primitive antiquity." Where members of alien lineage were taken into the fold it was at least on the basis of a legal fiction that they were "descended from the same stock as the people on whom they were engrafted." [1]

When Lewis H. Morgan developed his own scheme of "Ancient Society" (1877), he not only adopted Maine's basic distinction but also gave greater definiteness to the views of his predecessor, especially in point of chronology. All forms of government, he argued, belonged to one of two categories—they were either founded on persons and personal relations or on territory and property. Ranged on one side were such units as the gens (clan, sib) and phratry; on the other, the series comprising the ward, township, county, province, and national domain. Political, that is, territorial organization was declared to have been unknown prior to classical antiquity. It was in 594 B.C. that Solon took the initial step of breaking up the patrilineal gentes (clans, sibs) of the Athenians by a property classification, and in 507 B.C. Cleisthenes completed the advance by substituting for the traditional gentile organization purely local lines of division, by cutting up the old noble lineages and assigning the fragments to different local groups. Henceforth every citizen was registered, taxed, and given a vote as a member not of a clan but of a township, that is, of a territorial unit.

This classical distinction between "social" or "tribal," and "political" or "territorial," organization is significant and unexceptionable. That is to say, there *is* a fundamental difference between the two principles discriminated, and of both the history of human society provides abundant examples. It is not the logical but the historical

[1] *Ancient Law*, Chapter V, pp. 124–26.

Selected Writings

aspect of the theory that evokes doubt. Why should the peoples of the world, after contentedly living for millennia under a government based on the blood tie, engage in that startling revolution described by Maine, of substituting the totally novel alignment of persons by locality? Neither author provides an adequate solution. Must we here break with the notion of continuous evolution? That certainly grates on the sensibilities of latter-day historical-mindedness. In the presence of overwhelming positive evidence we should be willing to cast Continuity on the rubbish heap of exploded fictions, but without such rigorous demonstration we shall do well to cling to it and seek an alternative interpretation. Nor is it difficult to outline the avenue of approach. If 507 or 594 B.C. does *not* mark an abrupt departure from past tradition, then older and simpler communities must have displayed the local bond along with the consanguineal tie. The two principles, in other words, however antithetical, are not of necessity mutually exclusive. It is then possible to satisfy the postulate of Continuity. We are no longer face to face with the miracle of a spontaneous generation but with the scientific problem of how an originally weak but perceptible territorial sentiment, at first subordinate to the blood tie, was intensified to the point of assuming the dominant rôle.

Whether this interpretation is warranted, is of course a question to be determined by empirical facts.

In fairness we must, first of all, concede that these yield considerable justification for the position maintained by Maine and Morgan. Again and again, in going over the descriptive literature of social anthropology, the reader must be struck by the prominence of personal relationship in governmental affairs, such as the administration of justice. What, for instance, is the significance of the blood feud, which outside of Africa is such a common mode of adjusting misunderstandings? From the present angle it is simply a negation of the state: it implies the doctrine that persons living in the same village or country are not by such juxtaposition jointly subordinate to some transcendent local authority but have claims upon and obligations to their kin only, each lineage standing toward any other in the same relationship as, say, the United States to France or

England—perhaps actually at amity, yet at any time potentially shifting into a state of avowed hostility.

The condition thus abstractly defined is best illustrated by a series of examples taken from different parts of the primitive world.

Let us begin with the Yurok of northwestern California. We have already commented on the smallness of their political units; at present we are concerned with their composition. Examining one of the typical hamlets, such as Weitspus on the Klamath River, we find an aggregation of less than 200 souls, the male population comprising mainly or exclusively blood kindred. The women generally come from other settlements; apart from this tendency to "local exogamy," the village is a self-contained, independent center of population lacking a sense of attachment to any equivalent units, or of subordination to a major whole, and to that extent comparable with an Andamanese camp. Of adjacent settlements in a group, one "was sometimes involved in a feud while another directly across the river looked on." Indeed, even within the hamlet itself a communal sense is lacking: the individual Weitspus recognizes no duty to his fellow townsfolk, no executive or judicial authority; his obligations are to his kin and his kin only, so that "all so-called wars were only feuds that happened to involve large groups of kinsmen, several such groups, or unrelated fellow townsmen of the original participants." Notwithstanding the complete absence of administrative and legal officials, the Yurok have a definite code of customary laws; yet all "rights, claims, possessions, and privileges are individual and personal, and all wrongs are against individuals. There is no offense against the community, no duty owing it, no right or power of any sort inhering in it." And, as a corollary to this proposition, punishment of a public character is likewise wanting. "Each side to an issue presses and resists vigorously, exacts all it can, yields when it has to, continues the controversy when continuance promises to be profitable or settlement is clearly suicidal, and usually ends in compromising more or less." [2]

This description is, *mutatis mutandis*, wholly applicable to the Angami Naga, who occupy the hills between Assam and Burma.

[2] Kroeber, *Handbook of the Indians of California*, pp. 3, 8–15, 20, 49.

Though living in a village, the Angami looks upon the sib (clan) as the real unit of organization. "So distinct is the clan from the village that it forms almost a village in itself, often fortified within the village inside in its own boundaries and not infrequently at variance almost amounting to war with other clans in the same village. Under normal circumstances there are sporadic riots due to the internal dissensions between the kin groups since in most disputes between two men of different clans the clansmen on each side appear as partisans and foment the discord." Even in times of war clan jealousies prove a disruptive force.[3]

Perhaps a still more striking illustration is supplied by the Ifugao of northern Luzon, precisely because these Philippine Islanders exemplify the paradox of an exceedingly complicated body of customary law coupled with a condition of virtual anarchy. Our principal source, Dr. R. F. Barton,[4] is quite clear-cut on the subject. He represents the natives as acting with complete disregard of any considerations outside of relationship. An individual owes support to his kindred against all other kin groups, and in proportion to the proximity of his relationship, while he is free from any obligations to the remainder of the local group. This group has no authorized official to arrange disputes between distinct bodies of kindred; there is merely a go-between with purely advisory functions. According to the author's explicit interpretation the political life of the Ifugao rests on consanguinity, and on consanguinity only.

The three examples cited in some measure justify the views of Maine and Morgan. Here are three peoples remote from one another and described by as many independent witnesses, whose testimony agrees as to the point at issue. Nevertheless, a closer scrutiny of the evidence reveals in each and every one of these instances that while the blood tie is the conspicuous one the local bond is by no means wholly in abeyance.

Let us begin by examining the Ifugao, on whom the descriptive material is most abundant. We find, first of all, that throughout

---

[3] J. H. Hutton, *The Angami Nagas*, p. 109.
[4] *Ifugao Law*, in Univ. of Cal. Pub. in Amer. Arch. and Ethnol. (1919), XV: 1–127.

Ifugao territory there is substantial agreement as to customary law. The principles on which a go-between intermediating between warring families renders his decision enjoy general acceptance, even though they may be warped in particular applications. In cases of adultery a fine is imposed on the offender, the amount varying with the relative status in society of the aggrieved and the guilty party. That *some* penalty should be inflicted is acknowledged even by the offender and his relatives; they are merely leagued together to shield him from bodily harm and beat down exorbitant demands for idemnity. Even if the adulterer is a prominent man supported by a host of henchmen he does not seek wholly to evade punishment but only to reduce it to a minimum. In short, there *is* definite recognition of some obligations to *un*related members of the same community. This rudimentary sense of duty toward the local group stands forth most clearly in the treatment of thieves. If Barton's picture of Ifugao society were to be taken literally, we should expect the same punishment to be meted out to *any* person outside the aggrieved party's kindred. But this inference does not tally with the facts reported. Theft committed by a fellow villager is mulcted by a traditional fine; a marauding outsider, however, is almost certain to be slain forthwith. Similarly, the principle of collective responsibility is extended beyond the circle of consanguinity so as to embrace the neighborhood group. If a creditor remains unsatisfied, he may on occasion appropriate buffalo belonging not only to his tardy debtor or his kin but those of any person inhabiting the same village.

Finally, there is a tacit understanding among different kin groups that internecine strife should be discountenanced lest the *territorial* unit be unduly weakened as compared with corresponding units; and the individual Ifugao is expected to comport himself in such fashion as not to entangle his neighbors in hostilities with other *local* groups. In short, the apparently exclusive potency of blood relationship is seen to be appreciably limited by the recognition of local contiguity as a basis for political action and sentiment.

What is true of the Ifugao, holds likewise for the equally "anarchic" Yurok. Professor Kroeber successfully disproves the existence of any *national* sentiment among them in his account of their so-

Selected Writings

called wars, which would fail to unite more than one tenth of the whole "tribe" against, say, the Hupa. But the same narratives also show that local affiliations of lesser scope were operative: "under threat of attack from a remote and consolidated alien foe, village might adhere to village in joint war, just as, in lesser feuds, town mates, impelled by bonds of association or imperiled by their common residence, would sometimes unite with the group of individuals with whom the feud originated." Our author adds that "these are occasions such as draw neighbors together the world over, be they individuals, districts, or nations." But that is precisely my contention, to wit, that even in extreme cases of separatism the neighborhood tie becomes a significant element in governmental activity, not perhaps in itself adequate for the institution of what we call "political" organization but providing the germ from which such an organization may develop.

This factor is strengthened by two features. For one thing, the men of a settlement are united by the institution of the sudatory, where they both sweat and sleep together throughout the winter and often in the summer, "passing the evenings in talk and smoking." The type of social unit thus created will be discussed more fully in the following chapter. Secondly, the local tie clearly appears in ritualistic activity. Not only is each ceremony riveted to a particular spot but, what is far more important in the present context, the association with localities serves to knit people together. Every main performance is conducted by competing parties representing as many villages. "These match and outdo one another, as the rich man of each village gradually hands over more and more of his own and his followers' and friends' valuables to the dancers to display." Moreover, it may be said that the very fact of such amicable rivalry in some manner counteracts the excessive particularism described above. It might have paved the way, though apparently among the Yurok it never did, for a more extensive union of local bodies.[5]

Angami conditions are amazingly like those reported for the Yurok and the Ifugao. On the one hand, the same centrifugal tendency is expressed in exaggeratedly tangible form, so that one

[5] Kroeber, *Handbook of the Indians of Califorma*, pp. 15, 50, 55, 81.

clan in the village may be separated from the rest by a wall twelve feet in thickness. Murder leads to a vendetta waged by the clans concerned rather than to the expulsion of the criminal by a judicial authority, and in cases of misunderstanding between persons of different villages the blood feud might be restricted to the kindred of the two parties "and it would be quite possible for all the other clans in both villages to be friendly, while the clans of the respective parties to the vendetta were on head-taking terms." Nevertheless, when a serious breach of the social code occurs "the clans in almost any village would be found agreed"; military operations are certainly carried on by villagers as such; and many important magico-religious observances are communal in character.[6]

The Yurok, Ifugao and Angami are *a fortiori* instances: they represent the maximum conceivable lack of governmental coördination of the kin groups occupying the same habitat. If even here the traditional theory of the exclusiveness of the blood tie breaks down, the presence of the local bond will have to be admitted for less extreme cases. However, it is possible to go further and to turn the tables on Maine and Morgan. Not only do local ties coexist with those of blood kinship, but it may be contended that the bond of relationship when defined in sociological rather than biological terms is itself in no small part a *derivative* of local contiguity. This view is so contrary to accepted notions that some evidence must be adduced in its defense.

Let us once more turn to the Angami Naga. Like many of the ruder peoples, they are divided into moieties, each child being reckoned from birth either a Pezoma or a Pepfüma according to his father's half of the tribe. This dual organization is traced to two legendary brothers, whose respective descendants the members of the two subdivisions are believed to be. But unlike such lineages elsewhere, the Angami moieties are not exogamous at the present time: often the population of a village is composed wholly of persons of one moiety and no objection is voiced against the marriage of fellow members. It is credibly stated by Mr. Hutton's informants that the customary taboo once held sway, but in course of time there seems

[6] Hutton, *The Angami Nagas*, pp. 45, 109, 150 *seq.*, 193.

Selected Writings

to have been a constant shift of the marriage regulating function to lesser and lesser fragments of the moiety. Thus, the village of Kohima is inhabited exclusively by Pepfüma people, who freely intermarry so far as they belong to distinct sibs. Of these, at one time within native tradition, there were only two, *viz.*, the Cherama and the Pferonoma. These, accordingly, were at that time to all intents and purposes exogamous moieties on the familiar pattern, as Pezoma and Pepfüma are reputed to have once been. But while Cherama persisted unsegmented, its mate was broken up into six sections, making (with Cherama) seven sibs in all at the present time. The exogamous unit of Kohima has thus been repeatedly redefined: at first it was presumably the archaic Pepfüma moiety, whose members were forced to seek spouses outside their own village; subsequently fellow-Pepfüma might marry, provided the union was that of a Cherama with a Pferonoma; and finally, a Pferonoma of sib *a* might marry either a Cherama or a Pferonoma of sibs *b, c, d, e, f*.

Nevertheless, so far there is no deviation from the widespread principle that marriage is regulated by *some* sort of kinship body, though the incest group, to use a convenient term, has materially shrunk in course of time. When, however, we scrutinize the data of Mr. Hutton's genealogical tables and his accompanying text, a new fact of the utmost importance emerges. *Permissible intermarriage is a function of locality no less than of consanguinity.* That is to say, the more inclusive kinship taboo is relaxed only insofar as the individuals concerned are not co-residents in the same community. To quote some striking sentences from our author's report:

"The marriage in the present generation is Pezoma-Pezoma, but *between different villages.*"

"Here there is a Pezoma-Pezoma marriage in the last generation and a Pepfüma-Pepfüma marriage in the generation before, but in the latter case *between persons of different villages.*"

The Cherhechima division "may not intermarry within itself *in the same village.*" [7]

The kin group, in short, is not a marriage regulating group simply

[7] Hutton, *Ibid.*, p. 110 *seq.*, pp. 125–32, 418 *seq.* The italics are mine.

because it is a kin group but partly, at least, because it is a local group.

This interpretation, however, may be challenged on the ground that the territorial factor came to be stressed at a relatively late stage, while in the earlier periods the patrilineal kin group was the sole principle regulating sex relations. It might also be contended that even today the intrusion of the local factor is incidental or derivative: exogamy is local only because within the settlement there is certainty as to blood kinship while people living elsewhere are either not known to be related or known to be only remotely related. This argument is plausible enough, and in order to meet it we must proceed to a critique of the kinship concept itself.

While kinship is universally recognized between a child and both his parents, this resulting "bilateral" kin group corresponding to our own family is frequently supplemented among the simpler peoples of the globe by the familiar "unilateral" kin. That is to say, the child is linked either with the father *or* the mother, the Angami illustrating the patrilineal, the Hopi of Arizona the matrilineal variety of unilateral reckoning. Since the bilateral family is omnipresent, this may seem to involve a contradiction, which, nevertheless, is more apparent than real. The bilateral family may, for instance, center in certain economic duties and sentimental attachments, while political functions—say, the blood feud—are connected solely with the patrilineal group.

Now, my contention is that both the bilateral (family) and the unilateral (clan, sib, moiety) unit are rooted in a local as well as a consanguine factor. Let us begin by considering the unilateral kin group, which in some quarters is still regarded as a distinguishing badge of primitive society generally.

Among the unilaterally organized tribes there are some in which the kin and the territorial group coincide. This is true of large sections of California. Mr. Gifford has recently shown that the Miwok, who live near the center of the state, were formerly split up into minute paternal lineages, each politically autonomous, each bearing a local name and owning a definite tract of land. Closely conforming to this model, the South Californian Diegueño were organized into patrilineal groups controlling areas so definitely circumscribed that it has been possible to plot their respective holdings. Similarly, in West Australia the local group embraces a body of blood relatives related through their fathers, and it is this small group, simultaneously consanguine and territorial, that acts as a miniature state, for example, by waging war.[8]

Now, what makes a group of this type cohere? It is easy to say that the sense of blood relationship is primary, but very difficult to prove; for what we observe is not such priority but the inextricable union of the consanguine and the local bond. Each unit in West Australia feels itself indissolubly linked with a definite locality by mystical ties. Why? Because of the reverence felt for the paternal ancestry settled there? But why *should* the paternal ancestry be singled out for reverential treatment? Is it not possible to invert the cheap and obvious explanation? It may be that the aborigines do not view a locality reverently because it is connected with their paternal ancestors but that they esteem their ancestors insofar as they are linked with a certain locality.

This leads us directly to the core of the clan problem. Why, we ask, do people ever feel a more special affiliation with one side of the family than with the other? It cannot be the kinship factor that accounts for the differential relationship, for that factor would operate equally for the paternal and the maternal kindred. The clue to the solution was long ago supplied by E. B. Tylor.[9] Let us assume the rule of marriage that obtains among the Hopi of Arizona —matrilocal residence. By this the bridegroom takes up his abode with his wife's parents, that is to say, since there is female house ownership, with his mother-in-law, to whom her other daughters likewise bring their several husbands. This explains forthwith why kinsfolk biologically on a par are discriminated sociologically. Between the mother's brother, who sees his sisters' children grow

---
[8] E. W. Gifford, *Miwok Lineages and the Political Unit in Aboriginal Californa*, in *American Anthropologist*, pp. 389–401. L. Spier, *Southern Diegueño Customs*, in *Univ. Cal. Publs. Amer. Arch. and Ethnol.* (1923), XX: 296–308. R. H. Lowie, *Primitive Society*, p. 393.
[9] "The Matriarchal Family System," in *Nineteenth Century* (1896), pp. 91–96.

up under his own mother's roof, and his nephews and nieces there naturally develops a sentiment of attachment that cannot possibly obtain between them and the father's brother. Similarly, the mother's sister becomes a closer relation than the paternal aunt, who cannot possibly be a co-resident. It is equally clear why there is a discrimination between different types of cousin. A Hopi grows up with the children of his mother's sister, while the children of his *father's* sister are reared in another house. In corresponding fashion the scales are weighted in favor of the *paternal* kin wherever patrilocal residence takes the place of matrilocalism. In short, spatial segregation accounts to a large extent for the alignment of relatives found in a tribe organized into clans.

It is true that residence after marriage is not always rigidly or permanently fixed, and in such cases supplementary factors must be invoked. For instance, a paternal lineage may be linked, as in northeastern North America, by common utilization of a hunting territory. Again, as in sections of Australia, a maternal kin group may cohere through exploitation of the same seed gathering tract; or, as among the Hidatsa, by the joint cultivation of a plot by a mother, her daughters, and her daughters' daughters. But in each of these instances, the ultimate determinant of cohesion is evidently not mere kinship but kinship enforced by propinquity.

So far I have considered the blood bond only with reference to the unilateral kinship group which looms so large in the discussions of ancient law. At present, however, it is recognized by all ethnologists open to argument that the unilateral principle is not a primeval one but was superimposed at a relatively late period upon the bilateral principle, which invariably accompanies it. The evidence from nearly all the unequivocally simplest tribes of the globe, such as the Shoshoneans of Utah and Nevada, the Yahgan of Tierra del Fuego, the Andamanese of the Bay of Bengal, and the Chukchi of northeastern Siberia, seems to dispose of the hoary dogma that the clan is a truly archaic institution.[10] If, then, the basic importance of the local element is to be established, it must be demonstrated

[10] R. H. Lowie, *Primitive Society*, p. 150 *seq.* W. Schmidt, *Völker und Kulturen*, p. 79 *seq.*

not only in association with the unilateral clan but also with the bilateral family.

The very attempt to do this may seem fantastic; for how can anything claim equal rank with those fundamental blood ties upon which our very existence depends? Here, however, we must stress a point of the utmost importance, which has been recently expressed by Dr. Malinowski. Biological and sociological kinship are two distinct concepts. The one is based on instinctive response in accordance with biological utility; the other, however dependent for its origin on the former, is never wholly derived from it and may diverge from it very appreciably. As Malinowski insists, the maternal *instinct* ceases with the discharge of its biological functions; it becomes a *sociologically* creative force only when it has ripened into a specifically human "sentiment" in Shand's sense of the term. But what is it, I should ask, that fosters the sentiment unless it is the constant association during childhood—prolonged in primitive communities by the generally extended period of lactation? Eliminate the element of contiguity, and the family as a *social* unit tends to disappear. Bogoras's graphic picture of Chukchi life introduces us to lone boys wandering away from home never to return. In what sense do they remain members of their families? Evidently only in a biological sense; sociologically the tie snaps when it fails to be reinforced by spatial proximity.

As for the bond between father and child, we have that whole range of usages which obscure biological paternity while in no way affecting the social or legal kinship. The case of the Bánaro, who live along the Potter's River in New Guinea, has been thoroughly elucidated by Dr. Thurnwald and may serve for purposes of illustration.[11] A Bánaro bride is not initiated into the mysteries of sex life by her husband, but by a friend of her husband's father and, subsequently, by her father-in-law. These activities take place in the so-called spirit hall of the village, and the men themselves are said to impersonate a spirit. As for the groom, he is not permitted access to his wife until after the birth of a child, which is designated as a

[11] Thurnwald, *Die Gemeinde der Bánaro* (Stuttgart, 1921), pp. 21 *seq.*, 37 *f.*, 99 *seq.*

"spirit's child" (*Geisterkind*) but is adopted by his mother's husband. Owing to the ceremonial laxity of sex relations during great tribal festivals, the husband cannot even be certain of his paternity in the case of subsequent issue. But, as our authority again and again assures us, this is a matter of complete indifference to the natives: "*Ob der Gatte der wirkliche Vater der Kinder ist, kommt bei diesem System nicht in Betracht.*" The concept of fatherhood is linked with that not of procreator but of educator, provider, and protector. It is the husband's cohabitation with the mother—in the etymological no less than in the customary sense of the term—that stamps him sociologically as a parent and makes the children members of *his* clan. Kinship is not kinship in its own right, but as a derivative of a local factor. As Dr. Malinowski has put it, there seems to be a "tendency in the human species, on the part of the male to feel attached to the children born by a woman with whom he has mated, has been living permanently and has kept watch over during her pregnancy." [12]

Dr. Thurnwald's Papuan case is but a special sample of the wider category of adoption—that legal fiction by which children who need not even be related may become, for all social purposes, as their adoptive parents' real offspring. Whatever may be the motive in different areas, which presumably varies considerably, the psychological concomitant is usually a sentimental relationship that approximates, if it does not attain, the natural emotions. The data from other areas seem to me to corroborate my personal impression among the Crow Indians, that there is a generic love of children—no matter whose—which merely requires to be particularized in a definite instance by constant association in order to develop into a full-fledged parental sentiment.

To sum up our argument. The traditional distinction established by Maine and Morgan retains its validity in so far as conceptually a union of neighbors is different from a union of kinsmen. It must even be conceded that the blood tie is frequently the overshadowing element in the governmental activities of primitive peoples. Yet, though it often dwarfs the territorial factor, it never succeeds in eliminating it. Nay, if we inquire into the bond of consanguinity

[12] B. Malinowski, *Crime and Custom in Savage Society* (1926), p. 107.

itself, we find lurking in the background a spatial determinant of the sentiments underlying it. Abstractly separated by a chasm, the two types of union are in reality intertwined. The basic problem of the state is thus not that of explaining the somersault by which ancient peoples achieved the step from a government by personal relations to one by territorial contiguity only. The question is rather to show what processes strengthened the local tie which must be recognized as not less ancient than the rival principle.

No collection of Lowie's writings would be complete without a selection from his work on the Indians of the northern Plains. Lowie knew an enormous amount of ethnography, but his knowledge of the Plains paled the rest of his erudition. He knew the area and its peoples with a thoroughness born of intensive reading, tenacious memory, extensive firsthand experience, and abiding love.

Lowie's interest in the origin of the state grew in part out of his knowledge of the military societies of the Plains (see also text pp. 65–71). He found in these associations, which exercised coercive, physical sanctions during certain periods, the seed of broader governmental institutions. He was well aware, however, of the temporary and situational limits of such powers, for a society that had the responsibility of policing the annual buffalo hunt might have no other enforcement privileges during the rest of the year. The nature of recruitment into the associations and their powers and obligations also varied from tribe to tribe, making generalizations about them difficult. This made them ideal subjects for Lowie, for he liked nothing better than to analyze a complex of activities found in a geographically contiguous area, but showing certain variations in both form and function from group to group. This allowed him to look for social determinants of the variations, as well as the similarities, as well as providing him with test cases of the historical influences of the tribes upon each other. He continually played similarity and difference one against the other, and for those who

Robert H. Lowie

found general laws in culture, Lowie always had a mountain of exceptions and limiting provisos. He thought with data and through data, for, to him, the facts always existed prior to the constructs.

Property Rights and Coercive Powers of Plains Indian Military Societies *

I

✣ Among the founders of comparative sociology Heinrich Schurtz deserves a lasting place of honor. Prior to his *Altersklassen und Männerbünde* (Berlin, 1902) the wide distribution and social significance of associations in primitive life had escaped the notice of theorists, who confined themselves largely to problems connected with marriage, the family, and the clan. Schurtz's pioneer effort was far from flawless. There are facile generalizations on the psychology of sex and irrelevant personal opinions that may be charged to the exhibitionism of youth. The author also misinterprets ethnographic evidence from sheer ignorance of the facts, which at that time were sadly wanting for many areas. Yet in historical perspective the book commands respect as one of the landmarks in the development of the science.[1]

One of Schurtz's cardinal postulates was the function of age differences as creators of social units: age-grades, he contended, were humanity's earliest *deliberate* attempt at social segmentation. Thus he naturally came to impress into service the remarkable information Prince Maximilian of Wied-Neuwied had collected among the Mandan and their neighbors of the upper Missouri in the early thirties of the last century.[2] For the Prince reported from each tribe

---

* *Journal of Legal and Political Sociology*, Vol. 1, pp. 59–71, 1943. Reproduced by permission of Philosophical Library. In a somewhat different form the second part of this paper was read at one of the Fiftieth Anniversary Symposia of the University of Chicago, September, 1941.

[1] For a critique, see R. H. Lowie, *Primitive Society*, Chapter XI.

[2] For a summary of these and later data see Clark Wissler, R. H. Lowie, *et al.*, Societies of the Plains Indians, constituting Volume XI of the Anthropological Papers of the American Museum of Natural History. This series will be cited hereafter as AMNH, followed by the number of the volume.

Selected Writings

a series of men's societies differentiated by emblems, songs, dances, behavior, and age. Growing older was not the sole basis of a higher membership, to be sure, since payments were prerequisite. But any thinker who assumed a normal sequence of stages in social development could easily dispose of the complication: Schurtz simply explained the Plains Indian phenomena as transitional from the earlier type of pure age-classes to the as yet unattained type of the pure club in which membership rests solely on payment of a fee.[3]

Field research subsequent to Schurtz and largely stimulated by his theories brought out a fact he could not have gleaned from Maximilian. Though specific societies were often closely paralleled in alien tribes, the pattern found by the Prince as underlying the entire tribal system of military organizations turned out to hold for only a bare half dozen Plains groups. Everywhere else societies were neither graded by age nor entered by payments. This in itself was no refutation of Schurtz's chronology: conceivably the rarer pattern might nevertheless be the older. However, the reverse assumption became *a priori* equally legitimate.

More vital was a discovery in part already to be gleaned from the earlier sources. A particular organization, such as the widespread Kit-fox society, was not indissolubly linked with a particular age: a young men's company on the upper Missouri, it ranked much higher in the Blackfoot (Montana, Alberta) scheme, and was of course coördinate with other organizations in the ungraded systems. Even within a single tribe the place of a military society varied with the lapse of time. Whereas Maximilian's Blackfoot in 1833 rated the Dogs as inferior to the Ravens, all subsequent observers reverse the order. Similarly, Curtis's Braves in the same tribe comprised the oldest bachelors, but according to Wissler they were predominantly young married men.[4] Membership in association A, B, C, . . . was therefore devoid of an intrinsic, immutable age status. Its basic meaning must be sought elsewhere.

The clue came through the disruptive agency of modern condi-

[3] Schurtz, *Alterklassen und Männerbunde*, 83 sq., 151–65.
[4] AMNH 11, 365–81. Among people who do not reckon their ages exactly by years, matrimonial status is significant in this context, as Schurtz recognized.

tions. Because of the ensuing upheaval, companies of men who would normally have jointly acquired a higher society failed to buy a new membership. It turned out that these men did not automatically rise to a higher grade, but remained in the societies they had bought. However, the native attitude went much further: in 1910 a Hidatsa (North Dakota) about 90 years old considered himself *simultaneously* a member of organizations joined at about seven, twenty, twenty-seven, and forty-five, respectively. Identical conceptions obtained among the Mandan (North Dakota) and Blackfoot.[5] The variations among the Arapaho (Wyoming) and Gros Ventre (Montana, Alberta) are negligible in this context, for they harmonize with the principle that membership in a graded society of the Plains was a form of negotiable property the claim upon which never lapsed until it was sold. The very tribes, then, which apparently stressed age-stratification in their graded series in actuality considered *purchase* as the basic principle of affiliation.

Whence, however, the empirically established fact that at any one time fellow-members were virtually all contemporaries? Here Schurtz stands vindicated. He erred, indeed, in asserting the necessary priority of associations uniting the age-mates of a community, but he was right in ascribing to coëvals the solidarity that could create social units and thereby differentiate them from one another. There is abundant evidence from our area that young boys were wont to foregather as a spontaneous, informal age-class in imitation of their elders. In tribes with a system of crystallized age-societies nothing would be more natural than for these boys collectively to buy the right to the lowest organized society, and later to continue buying successive memberships at suitable intervals. We must distinguish, then, two senses of the term "society." On the one hand, we are dealing with sets of incorporeal property rights. Any one complex was not intrinsically linked with a particular age grade, so that shifts in point of age occurred either through internal rearrangements or when a society was borrowed (or bought) by an alien group. On the other hand, the gang of united youngsters would regularly remain

---

[5] *Ibid.*, 427, 972–75.

together and subsequently buy their way up to the top of the scale. These age-mates, then, do form a body independent of their joint property rights; for during the interval between their sale of a particular membership and their purchase of another their sense of solidarity would persist unabated even though joint activity might dwindle to a minimum.

This distinction appears most clearly among the Gros Ventre (Montana, Alberta), where each gang bore a unique name but shared a set of "dance" privileges with several other gangs, i.e., with adjoining age-groups which performed like dances with like regalia, but always independently of one another. Thus, a man for a lifetime labeled as a Holding-to-a-dog's-tail was reckoned a Dog only during and after the performance of the Dog ceremony, sharing *that* appellation with the other gangs owning the same prerogatives.[6]

As to the property rights of the age-societies in general, several points are worth noting. As just explained, several groups might equally share in the "copyright" to a particular complex. To a more limited extent other tribes than the Gros Ventre permitted the sharing of the same emblems or other integral parts of complexes by distinct bodies. This fact might also be phrased by saying that the same item could enter distinct complexes. Furthermore, both the acquisition of membership and the rights obtained were only in part collective. A Hidatsa gang jointly made a large soliciting gift to a higher group in order to coax them into selling their society; but subsequently each buyer might have an individual seller as his ceremonial "father," obtaining by the transaction distinctive privileges such as go with honorific offices. Finally, there are the tribes with ungraded systems and without purchase. Here, e.g., among the Crow (Montana), one gang did not replace another, but individuals spontaneously joined or were invited to add to the numerical strength of a society. Undeniably the members here also had property rights: these could be lost, as when one of two rival Crow organizations excelled the other in martial exploits and thereby won the right to monopolize the losers' tunes for one season. However, from the legal

[6] *Ibid.*, 933. A. L. Kroeber, "Ethnology of the Gros Ventre," AMNH 1, 232, 1908.

point of view, it is an important matter whether possessions are, or are not, negotiable: Inalienable land is property in a different sense from land that can be disposed of at will.

The curious point in this connection is that the tribes in question are by no means unfamiliar with the concept of selling incorporeal property, such transactions being in fact a constantly recurring phenomenon among the Crow (Montana), who used to pay a horse even for such minor privileges as painting the cheeks with a certain design. Why, then, did they fail to extend so deep-rooted a conception to their military societies? Without generalizing for the entire area I should suggest the following explanation for the Crow. These Indians did sell a variety of privileges, but these come exclusively, or at least preponderantly, into the category of *sacred* possessions, i.e., they were directly or indirectly traced to supernatural revelations. But their military societies were devoid of religious meaning; a few extremely faint reminiscences of visionary experiences to explain the origin of certain organizations could not arrest their thoroughgoing secularization. The complex of badges, songs, and activities of a military society was thus valued quite differently from the corresponding complex of the sacred Tobacco societies and fell into a distinct category in Crow consciousness.

II

For a large portion of our area and adjoining regions to the east and north early sources attest a minimum of governmental authority. Denig's description of an Assiniboine council, Tanner's account of a joint enterprise by Ojibwa (Great Lakes), Cree (Central and Western Canada), and Assiniboine (Western Canada, Montana), Tabeau's observations among the Dakota and Arikara (North Dakota), Hearne's experiences with his Chipewyan (Athabaska-Mackenzie area) guide, Matonabbee, are all mutually corroboratory on this point. According to Jones's summary of aboriginal Ojibwa conditions, e.g., there were counselors with narrowly localized jurisdiction to which status every tribesman was admissible. Their powers were vague and limited, and the chief chosen by them was even less able to alter existing custom at his pleasure. In Denig's day the head chief of the Assiniboine was a purely nominal leader who lacked special prerogatives and could be humiliatingly overruled by the council. The chiefs known to Tabeau were unable to quell a riot and might have their authority set at nought by a single resolute individual: "insubordination and discord" reigned supreme.[7]

Making due allowance for exaggerations we find concordant testimony, perhaps not for the anarchy implied in some of the statements if taken literally, but at least for a marked freedom of the individual from physical restraint. This impression is strengthened by the widely held definition of ideal public functionaries. The Pawnee (Nebraska) chief, far from being a sovereign ruler, was above all a peacemaker and guardian of the village, his Hidatsa colleague was "a man of general benevolence who offered smoke to the old people and feasted the poor." Their counterpart among the Plains Cree was not only expected to exercise generosity, but to sacrifice his property for the maintenance of order, nay, to forgo vengeance if one of his own kinsmen was slain. Correspondingly, a Winnebago (Wisconsin) chief constantly distributed his possessions and interceded between evildoers and their revengeful victims; he went so far as to mortify his own flesh in order to arouse the pity of the aggrieved, thus deflecting their anger from the culprits. In these tribes, then, the chief was essentially an appeaser working by cajolery. Small wonder that his adjutants and what has been called the camp police operated under like restrictions. The duty of all Plains Cree of superior status was to prevent strife; and the Black Mouths of an Hidatsa village removed misunderstandings, conciliating aggrieved tribesmen by gentle words and compensatory gifts.[8]

---

[7] E. Th. Denig, Indian Tribes of the Upper Missouri, *in* 46th Ann. Rept., Bureau of American Ethnology, 431 sq., 435–440, 449 (1930). This series will hereafter be quoted as BAE, followed by the serial number of the reports. Edwin James, editor, An Indian Captivity (1789–1822); John Tanner's Narrative of his Captivity among the Ottowa and Ojibwa Indians, 1830 (Sutro Branch, Calif. State Library, Reprint Series, No. 20, chapter XI, 151). Annie Heloise Abel, Tabeau's Narrative of Loisel's Expedition to the Upper Missouri (Norman, Okla., 1939), 104–106, 126. William Jones, Central Algonkin, *in* Ann. Arch. Rept. for 1905 (Toronto, 1906), 137. Samuel Hearne, Journey from Prince of Wales Fort in Hudson's Bay to the Northern Ocean (London, 1795), *passim*.
[8] G. A. Dorsey and J. R. Murie, Notes on Skidi Pawnee Society, *in* Anthro-

Robert H. Lowie

In view of these facts it is startling to find the liberties of the Plains Indian periodically suspended by something very much like martial law enforced by a body vested with supreme power for the time being. Probably the earliest report is Hennepin's. In 1680 the explorer met a Santee Dakota (Western Woodlands) party, who freely shared their recently obtained supply of buffalo meat. Suddenly:

Fifteen or sixteen Savages came into the middle of the Place where we were, with their great Clubs in their Hands. The first thing they did was to over-set the Cabin of those that had invited us. Then they took away all their Victuals, and what Bears-Oil they could find. . . .

We knew not what these Savages were at first. . . . One of them . . . told me, that those who had given us Victuals, had done basely to go and forestal the others in the Chase; and that according to the Laws and Customs of their Country, 'twas lawful for them to plunder them, since they had been the cause that the Bulls were all run away, before the Nation could get together, which was a great injury to the Publick; For when they are all met, they make a great Slaughter amongst the Bulls; for they surround them so on every side that 'tis impossible for them to escape.[9]

Tabeau, who was particularly familiar with the Arikara and Teton Dakota, tells us that the "soldiers" when elected "to watch over the carrying out of the laws of the *cerne* [buffalo surround] or over that of some public decision," have the right—only temporarily, he emphasizes—"to be severe arbitrarily towards every delinquent, to kill his dogs, his horses, to break his weapons, to tear the lodges into

---

pological Series, Field Museum of Natural History, 27:113 (1940). R. H. Lowie, Notes on the Social Organization and Customs of the Mandan, Hidatsa, and Crow Indians, AMNH 21:18 f. (1917). David G. Mandelbaum, The Plains Cree, AMNH 37:221, 230, 231 f. (1940). Paul Radin, The Winnebago Tribe, BAE 37:209 f., 227 (1923).

[9] L. Hennepin, A New Discovery of a Vast Country in America . . . (London, 1698), 187 f.

Selected Writings

tatters, and to seize . . . upon all that which belongs to him." [10] This corresponds well to the composite picture from a variety of sources on different groups. One would merely like to add that though a refractory culprit might be severely beaten and even killed, a penitent was rewarded with a new lodge and more goods than had been destroyed. Tabeau admits other public functions, but is particularly impressed with the direction of the collective hunt (*c'est surtout le cas ou les soldats sont séveres dans l'execution de leur charge*) and justifies the law as absolutely necessary because to transgress would be to "*detruire ainsi la base de la subsistance générale* (sic)."

It was observations of this type that I once combined with principles enunciated by Schurtz into an hypothesis for the evolution of the State. My problem was to account for the rise of territorial sovereignty from a condition in which, as earlier theorists had averred, kinship provided the only bond for joint political action. Schurtz himself had already argued that a closely knit primitive secret organization could inject order into communal life such as transcended the power of weak chiefs or was precluded by the constant bickering of rival clans.[11] Among the best known Plains peoples the temporary coercive authority was generally vested in military organizations, one or more of which units were empowered to punish the crime of stampeding buffalo. Thus, these Plains associations seemed a potential instrumentality for territorial integration, achieving intermittently, i.e., during the surround, what a modern State professes to do continuously. Subsequently the hostilities among the several associations within a tribe made a strong impression upon me and their mere existence appeared as potentially no less disruptive than that of contending blood groups. Nevertheless, I retained the idea that the hunt-directing police force illustrates "the meteoric display of sovereign authority" in "an almost anarchic community." [12]

Naturally the question obtrudes itself why an approach to com-

---

[10] Abel, Tabeau's Narrative . . . , 116 sq., 245.
[11] Heinrich Schurtz, *Alterklassen und Männerbünde*, 363, *et passim*. R. H. Lowie, *Primitive Society*, New York, 1920; *id.*, *The Origin of the State*, New York, 1927.
[12] Lowie, *The Origin of the State*, 107 sq., 116.

plete freedom should thus alternate with subjection to coercive force. For this there readily suggested itself an answer in economic terms. Securing an ample supply of buffalo meat was a matter of life and death, hence under the threat of starvation the Indians willingly surrendered their normal rights, subjecting themselves to a rigorous discipline.

In recent years Drs. Hoebel and Provinse have independently criticized my position.[13] They have not, however, rejected my specimens of compulsion as spurious, nor do they consider them irrelevant to the problem of political development. The gist of their comments is rather that I have understated the case: "Sovereignty"—to use a grandiloquent term which I invest with no fetishistic reverence in this context—is, they argue, less sporadic and more inclusive than my exposition suggests. It was misleading to overemphasize the spectacular disciplinary concomitants of the buffalo hunt. My own field data, as well as those of other observers, are aptly cited to show that the same procedures held in several distinct circumstances.

I accept the criticism as valid and should like to strengthen it by additional evidence. At the same time I must qualify some of its implications.

Ethnographic facts that contravene the unique significance of the buffalo surround come from the area to the east of the Plains. As Skinner and Macleod have noted,[14] several Woodland peoples, i.e., peoples for whose economy buffalo-hunting was a subordinate or even negligible feature, paralleled the phenomena so strikingly manifested by their western neighbors. The Winnebago constabulary did control the chase, but—like the Menomini (Wisconsin) counterpart

[13] E. Adamson Hoebel, Associations and the State in the Plains, in American Anthropologist 38:433–438, 1936; id., The Political Organization and Law-Ways of the Comanche Indians (Memoirs of the American Anthropological Association, No. 54, 1940), 82. John H. Provinse, The Underlying Sanctions of Plains Indian Culture, in Fred Eggan, ed., Social Anthropology of North American Tribes (Chicago, 1937), 365.
[14] Alanson Skinner, Social Life and Ceremonial Bundles of the Menomini Indians, AMNH 13:22–26, 1913; id., Material Culture of the Menomini (New York, 1921), 51 f.; id., Political Organization, Cults, and Ceremonies of the Plains—Ojibway and Plains Cree Indians, AMNH 11:498 f. (1914). Paul Radin, The Winnebago Tribe, BAE 37: 114, 209, 220, 226 f.

—they also proceeded in similar fashion to forestall premature exploitation of wild rice. The Sauk and Fox (Wisconsin) "war chiefs" directed not the hunt itself, but the homeward journey from it, their aim being to preclude hostile attacks on single families and the pillaging of corn by nimble marauders. Every night one war chief would set up his staff as a boundary mark, and whoever stepped beyond it had "his canoe and whatever else he may have along with him destroyed." As soon as the village routine was restored this martial law lapsed; in no other circumstance did our authority discover "any laws enforced or penalties exacted for disobedience of them." The Winnebago police had a variety of functions beyond those already mentioned. Besides preventing a stampede of game and premature inroads on wild rice, they regulated travel in the Sauk and Fox fashion, guarded the village continuously, and whipped seducers of women. Oddly enough, in cases of murder these coercers figured as appeasers.

It seems idle to speculate whether the police institution as we find it in the Plains originated there or in the Woodlands, especially since we know that many of the "Plains" tribes emigrated to their historic homes from the forested regions in relatively recent times. But it is evident that coercive functions are not indissolubly tied up with the conditions of hunting herds of big game. As indicated, they coexist with radically distinct pursuits. Further, they do not automatically arise from the buffalo surround. For the Sarsi (Alberta), the Comanche (Texas), the Shoshone (Idaho, Wyoming), marginal but in many ways thoroughly acclimatized representatives of the Plains, hence devoted buffalo hunters, either lacked punitive measures or reduced them to a minimum.[15]

Hoebel's and Provinse's criticisms are therefore well taken; the range of coercive powers did not coincide with buffalo hunting but embraced various other aspects of tribal life in the Plains and adjoining regions. As already indicated, this revision involves at bottom not a refutation but a strengthening of my basic contention, for it

---

[15] Diamond Jenness, The Sarcee Indians of Alberta, National Museum of Canada, Bulletin 90 (Ottawa, 1938), Anthrop. Ser., No. 23, 11, 41. Demitri Shimkin, personal communication concerning the Wind River Shoshone. Hoebel (1940), 82.

Robert H. Lowie

asserts a far broader base than the narrow economic one envisaged by me.

Though this is very gratifying, I must turn devil's advocate against the possible implication that the police phenomena demonstrate more than incipient Statehood. On the one hand, as explained above, the genuinely authoritarian aspects of various tribal constabularies (Crow, Winnebago) are superseded by purely persuasive functions in so vital a crisis as intratribal murder.

Secondly, we must recognize the seasonal dichotomy of social life among many Plains tribes, roughly paralleling the contrasts emphasized by Durkheim for the Australians and by Mauss for the Eskimo.[16]

Wissler stated the facts long ago,[17] pointing out the intermittent character of governmental control in our area, but my previous publications fail to give due emphasis to the data. A few representative phenomena may be cited. The Blackfoot held their council in the summer, separated after the fall hunt, and reassembled in the spring. Hidatsa villages were under a winter chief whose term began in autumn and ended with the melting snow. The Dakota and the Crow reorganized their military societies every spring and these companies functioned until the first snowfall. Three recent monographs bring out the essential point with startling clarity. For the Cree, the Sarsi, and the Kiowa (Oklahoma) social life culminated in the annual Sun Dance. It was for that ceremony that Cree bands would unite in the summer, soon thereafter dispersing and finally, in midwinter, breaking up into minute family groups too small to permit associational activity. Similarly, the Sarsi hunted buffalo in small tribal segments, and only for the Sun Dance one society, the Red Paint organization, assumed control. Again the Kiowa associations "functioned only during the four or so weeks of the Sundance gathering." [18]

---

[16] Marcel Mauss, Essai sur les variations saisonnières des sociétés Eskimo; étude de morphologie sociale, *in* L'Année Sociologique, 9:39–132, 1906. Emile Durkheim, *Les formes élementaires de la vie religieuse* (Paris, 1912), *passim*.
[17] Clark Wissler, *The American Indian* (New York, 1922), pp. 161, 178.
[18] Wissler, *The Social Life of the Blackfoot Indians*, AMNH 7:22–26 (1911); id., in AMNH 11:24 (1912). Lowie, op. cit., in AMNH 21:18 f. (1917). Man-

Selected Writings

The lapse of authoritarianism for a considerable, or in some tribes, even the major part of the year as a result of economic conditions and consequent modes of settlement, inevitably reduces whatever sovereignty exists to a nascent stage.

Finally, as Provinse aptly shows, there may be dispersal of authority between two or even more agencies. For example, normally during the season of reunion the Crow camp would be under the guidance of a chief and the military society appointed by him; but at a Sun Dance the director of that ceremony is supreme and appoints another association to serve for its duration.[19] Such temporal alternation of supreme power evidently militates against the centralization of authority.

However suggestive, then, the data on police functions in and near our area are, they suggest nascent rather than achieved governmental integration. The failure to extend the coercive authority of police associations over the entire field of internal relations (notably in the case of murder); the merely periodic, in some cases even ephemeral, assumption of such authority; its dispersal between two or more foci; the disruptive tendency of strife between rival associations pointed out in *The Origin of the State*—all militate against the creation of a full-fledged State.

Nevertheless, the potential jurisdiction of a military society remains a most significant fact for our theme. This has been very effectively demonstrated for the Cheyenne (Montana). Although here, too, the seasonal dichotomy breaks up the societies during the fall and winter, this did not apply to the Dogs, who by an historical accident coincided with one of the tribal bands, hence preserved a unique solidarity. In fact, some semblance of cohesion obtained even in the other societies inasmuch as members who happened to reside together during the period of dispersal might join in action as occasions arose. Possibly most illuminating is a case of mayhem. Among Plains Indian peoples generally such an offense was only a tort, the police assuming the function of mere go-betweens in trying

---

delbaum, op. cit., 203, 225. Jenness, op. cit., 11, 41 f. Jane Richardson, Law and Status among the Kiowa Indians (New York, 1940), 9 f.
[19] Lowie, *The Crow Indians* (New York, 1935), p. 308.

to persuade the aggrieved party to accept an indemnity. Here, however, something radically different occurred: the Foxes then serving as police treated the matter as a public wrong, severely beat the culprit, and accepted the "fine" offered by him without sharing it with his victim.[20] This certainly suggests that the governmental powers of a military organization were capable of very considerable enlargement.

One question which remains is whether the germs of sovereignty were peculiarly tied up with the rise of military associations. Reverting to the ethnographic correction made above concerning the supposedly unique effect of the buffalo surround, I should like to point out that the geographical extension of our police phenomenon automatically supplies an answer. For in the Woodlands there are no military societies of either the graded or ungraded type. Moreover, it has long been recognized that the conventional "Plains Indians" comprise a congeries of culturally disparate groups. Some are matrilineal, others patrilineal, still others without definite rules of descent. In one sector of the area kinship nomenclature is of the Omaha type, almost exactly duplicated in the western Woodlands; in another we find its precise logical antithesis, whose closest parallels crop up in the Southeast and in Arizona; still another province displays a third pattern. Agriculture is totally unknown to some tribes, rudimentary among others, more highly developed among the Pawnee. The Sun Dance, the dominant festival of the high Plains, dwindles to insignificance or disappearance among Southern Siouans, who in part substitute an equivalent of the Woodland ceremonial dramatizing the ritual killing and revival of initiates. These facts long ago recognized in conversation by the late Alanson Skinner have at last been adumbrated taxonomically by the suggestion of a "Wisconsin-Prairie" area.[21]

Now within the Prairie subdivision of this area we discover a fea-

[20] K. N. Llewellyn and E. Adamson Hoebel, *The Cheyenne Way* (Norman, Okla., 1941), Chapter V, esp. 99–101, 110 f., 115, 118 f., 115, 118 f., 122 ff.
[21] A. L. Kroeber, "Cultural and Natural Areas of Native North America," *in* University of California Publications in American Archaeology and Ethnology, 38:85 (1939).

ture shared not only with the complementary Wisconsin sector, but with a variety of still more easterly Woodland tribes: public functions of one sort or another devolve on the *clan*. Thus, it is the Bear clan that policed a Winnebago village, where, incidentally, the chief as an appeaser belonged to another, the Thunderbird, clan. This does not necessarily mean that all adult men of a certain clan formed the permanent police or that all the members of a squad were clansmen; the point is rather that at least the responsibility for recruiting and supervising the police rested upon one of more specific clans. Thus, the two Osage (Missouri) chiefs, each representing one of the two moieties and a particular "gens," i.e., patrilineal clan, within it, appointed the marshals for the hunt, one from each of certain gentes; and honorific titles devolved on three of the officers, each representing one of these units. Similarly, among the Iowa "the Elk gens furnished the soldiers or policemen"; and according to Fletcher and La Flesche, two clans were associated with the regulation of the hunt among the Ponca[22] (Nebraska).

The recruiting of a constabulary from definite clans is not, however, the only alternative to identifying it with a particular military association. Several Plains tribes used the device of what may be called a "nonce police." The Pawnee, for example, though vesting disciplinary powers within the village in the hands of the chief's adjutant and three appointees of his, regulated the buffalo hunt on a different principle, a priest selecting one of four possible organizations *for that particular enterprise only*. So the Omaha council would delegate to men from the class of brave warriors the task of controlling some communal hunt. The appointees formed no permanent body, but owing to their fitness were likely to be subsequently drafted for police duties in the village. From sources on the Plains Ojibwa, Dakota, and Assiniboine it seems probable that wherever men of recognized valor formed a distinct class they were the obvious candidates for constabulary duty. In short, *any* pre-existing unit clearly defined in native consciousness, whether military club, clan,

[22] Francis La Flesche, The Osage Tribe, BAE 36:66–68 (1921). J. O. Dorsey, Siouan Sociology, *in* BAE 15:238 (1897). Fletcher and La Flesche, op. cit., 45, 210, 279.

or distinguished warrior group, readily lent itself to such assignment.[23]

Summarizing the above remarks, I still feel that the military organizations of the Plains area exemplify the potentialities of associations as regards the creation of supreme central authority. It is merely necessary to remember that such germs of Statehood actually as a rule remained rudimentary, though the Cheyenne case demonstrates that some tribes carried them much nearer to fruition than others. Further, this type of unit is obviously not peculiarly fit to absorb disciplinary functions. Where military societies are lacking, such activities quite as naturally devolve on other pre-existing units, such as clans or a general honorary class of braves.

Note. For the orientation of the reader I list alphabetically the location of Indian tribes mentioned above. Where the habitat changed repeatedly in historic times, one or two significant locations are taken to suffice for present purposes.

Arapaho—Colorado, Wyoming
Arikara—N. Dakota
Assiniboine—Montana, Alberta
Blackfoot—Montana, Alberta
Cheyenne—Montana
Chipewyan—Hudson Bay to Lake Athabaska
Comanche—Colorado to Texas
Cree (Plains)—Manitoba to Alberta
Crow—Montana
Dakota (Santee)—Minnesota
Dakota (Teton)—S. Dakota
Fox—Wisconsin
Gros Ventre—Montana, Alberta
Hidatsa—N. Dakota
Iowa—Iowa
Kiowa—Oklahoma
Mandan—N. Dakota
Menomini—Wisconsin
Ojibwa—Great Lakes Region
Omaha—Nebraska
Osage—Missouri
Pawnee—Nebraska
Ponca—Nebraska
Sarsi—Alberta
Sauk—Wisconsin
Shoshoni—Wyoming, Idaho
Winnebago—Wisconsin

[23] Dorsey and Murie, Notes on Skidi Pawnee Society, 113. J. O. Dorsey, Omaha Sociology, in BAE 3:216 f., 233 f., 288, 321, 363 (1884). Alice C. Fletcher and Francis La Flesche, The Omaha Tribe, BAE 27:210, 279 (1911). James, op. cit., Chapter XII. Denig, Indian Tribes of the Upper Missouri, 436. Lowie in AMNH 11:132–136.

Selected Writings

This last in our series of essays by Lowie was written toward the end of his life and published posthumously. It is a gentle and charming discursion into life, the problem of meaning, and the importance of dream in the sustenance of hope (cf. pp. 71-74, above). He tells us of the uncompromising rationalism of his upbringing, the gradual mellowing of his views during the experience of field work, and his own discovery, as a scientist, of the vital role of religion in culture. Lowie wrote: "A living faith serves to integrate the individual's behavior in society, to give him confidence in meeting the crises that life inescapably brings and to introduce into his existence a stable central core in the light of which he can assign values."

Lowie remained a rationalist and a scientist, however, although he felt that science was beyond the needs and understanding of most men. Religion and science served different functions: religion sought peace, science truth. Ernst Mach, in the end as in the beginning, expressed Lowie's view: "The scientist's highest philosophy consists precisely in bearing an incomplete world-view and preferring it to one that is apparently complete, but inadequate." This expresses exactly Lowie's orientation toward anthropological theory.

Religion in Human Life *

✤ Since this article is concerned with the moot matter of religion, I should perhaps begin by making clear my own point of view and my reasons for coming to the conclusions that I have come to. My first awareness of religious strife came from my grandfather before I left Vienna at the age of ten; he had been an agnostic from his medical student days, and he laid the foundations for my own later attitudes. From my parents I received no religious training of any kind. By the time I was sixteen, I was already reading the *philosophes* and imitating their violent anticlericalism and bitterness toward all religion. This period continued, largely under the stimulus of and

---

* Reproduced by permission of the American Anthropological Association from *American Anthropologist*, Vol. 65, no. 3, pp. 532-42, 1963. This article was found among Professor Lowie's papers after his death on September 21, 1957.

acquaintance with Ernst Haeckel, until I was about twenty-five. At this point I was already going into the field as an ethnologist. It did not take long to discover that to the primitive mind religion was of paramount importance. If I wanted to understand the Indians of that period I simply had to study its values for them. Moreover, my constant field trips brought me into contact with dedicated men of all faiths who were certainly deriving neither money nor reknown by being missionaries to a group of Indians on a remote reservation. They lived as other members of the community did, in poverty, and they remained with their charges through pestilence and famine. One day it occurred to me that both the Indians and the hardy souls who were trying to convert them to Christianity had some inner strength that I lacked. Nor was I unique in this lack. I began to wonder how many scientists would undergo for their science the years of poverty that the priests and ministers willingly accepted for their religion.

Here clearly was a phenomenon of both primitive and civilized life that warranted study. So I began to collect information about native religions on the same objective basis upon which I assembled data on basket weaving, social organization, hunting, or any other aspect of primitive life. Moreover, through my reading I discovered that no group of people had ever been found who did not have a religion of some kind. Since religion is a universal manifestation, it must have some value. I found also that despite the immense variations in the outward observances, the inner glow and the function of religion in the group were identical from one form to another. The Catholic priest, the Mormon missionary, the Eskimo shaman, the African witch-doctor, and the Protestant clergyman were all alike in their sense of inner conviction, in their intense desire to help others, and in their dependence upon some force outside themselves that gave them courage. Fanatic, ignorant, or rigid they might be, but they were men of faith. I cannot say that I have become a religious man as the result of my study, but I have become an informed one; and I have seen too much to believe now in the dicta that I accepted in my youth. I no longer doubt that religion has a definite place in human life.

Selected Writings

My position toward religion as a cultural phenomenon springs directly from my conception of anthropology as a *science*. Since it is a science it must take cognizance of values because these form an essential part of its subject matter; but it must treat these values objectively—that is, it must refrain from judgment. Thus, an anthropologist who is studying West African fetishism must stick to what he can see and hear for himself and what he can find out from informants as to the meaning of fetishism to them, but he must not judge it in terms of his own religious standards. Probably my own lack of religious training was an asset rather than a drawback, because I could not condemn any form of worship merely because it differed from mine. I could only view it as a human manifestation worthy of scientific investigation. This same point of view should certainly be extended to include the religions of one's own day. Yet I have known anthropologists who accorded a benevolent understanding to the Hopi but denied it to Catholics, Mormons, Buddhists or Mohammedans. This dichotomy of viewpoint strikes me as ridiculous and completely unscientific. In short, I will study as many religions as I can, but I will judge none of them. I doubt if any other attitude is scientifically defensible.

To a modern intellectual, religion is probably the most unfamiliar subject in the world. He cannot, of course, remain wholly ignorant of its role in the past, but the sentiments of such men as St. Francis of Assisi, George Fox, or John Wesley are utterly remote and unintelligible. For many people the religious isssue is intertwined with an adolescent revolt against parental authority or with a struggle for intellectual freedom. For others it has become a symbol of restriction, repression, and reaction. To others it is either just plain mumbo jumbo or a narcotic. The former attitude is well illustrated by Voltaire's statement that religion began when the first knave duped the first fool. Marxians have their special brand of the second attitude: that it is an opiate with which exploiting capitalists lull the masses in order to fleece them wih impunity. Most if not all of these attitudes are based upon a profound ignorance of what religion is and does.

While it is true that religion has lost ground during the past century, it has never ceased to sway the lives and fortunes of millions. And even if open allegiance to a church has become more rare as the decades have flowed past, the moral strength of religion has continued to influence people. During World War II many people either found religion for the first time or else returned to their former church for comfort and strength to bear the fears and pressures brought about by war. It should never be forgotten that all religions thrive on adversity. It is probable that the common attitude of indifference and apathy is caused primarily by too much prosperity.

The indifference is not confined to one church or to one country, as may be seen from the following two examples. In Italy the vast majority of the population is Catholic. Some of the people are certainly devout, but these come predominantly from the peasant class. The others—excluding a handful of freethinkers—are passive in their Catholicism. They have their children baptized by the Church; they are married and buried by the Church; but they seem to go through life without religious feeling or spiritual experience.

The situation is much the same in Protestant Sweden, where the people are overwhelmingly Lutheran and the king is constitutionally bound to profess the evangelical creed. But when one glances through a brief survey of Swedish life, one finds a good deal about the iron and match industries, about timbering and handicrafts, and about sports, but strangely little concerning the officially dominant faith as a force in shaping human lives. In the newspapers the sporting page, though shorter than in American dailies, is easily three times as long as the half-page or less that has to do with church or religion.

It was not of course like this in medieval Europe. Art, scholarship, philosophy, education, and crafts of every sort were all permeated by the Church. And the earlier crusades bear witness to the dynamic power of the Christian faith among the people. This all-pervasive character of religion has almost vanished from contemporary life, but in the days of my field work I found it still alive among the Indians whom I visited. For instance, when the Choctaw played an intervillage game, the performance started on the previous evening

Selected Writings

with twelve repetitions of a ceremonial dance by the players. The tribal prophets continued their magic rites throughout the night, and during the game itself the conjurers were almost as conspicuous as the players. The most matter-of-fact features in the daily routine of any primitive people are likely to be linked with magical observances, prayers, chants, or sacrifices. In New Zealand a Maori recited sacred spells when he began to build a canoe, when he launched it, when he planted his crops, when he harvested them; even when he taught a youngster to weave, he muttered a charm to increase the learner's receptiveness. During their farming period the Apinayé of Northern Brazil sang daily songs in honor of the sun. The Eskimo firmly believed that success in sealing hinged upon the favor of a powerful sea goddess. And so forth ad infinitum all over the savage world.

The field worker's business is always and everywhere to understand the true inwardness of the beliefs and practices of the people he studies. He is not content to record that infants are suffocated, aged parents abandoned, or enemies eaten. Unless he can also recover the accompanying sentiments, he has failed in his task. It is one thing if a parent throttles his newborn child from sheer brutality, another if he kills it because the mother died in delivery and a nurse cannot be found, and still another if his tribe has a superstitious fear of twins. And the field worker who consistently sees human civilization as one indivisible whole cannot logically apply a sympathetic attitude to Australian infanticide, Eskimo abandonment of old people, or Tupinamba cannibalism, and a prejudiced attitude to Catholics, Baptists, or Methodists. The touchstone of his anthropological conscience is whether or not he treats the communicant of some other faith than his own with the consideration he professionally metes out to an Indian medicine man or an Eskimo shaman.

In my own field experience the Hopi of Arizona and the Crow of Montana both impressed upon me the integrating power of religion, but from two instructively antithetical angles. The Pueblos illustrate ceremonialism par excellence, with a profusion of outward observances and paraphernalia. What first of all amazes the observer among the Hopi is the incredible amount of time consumed by their religious activities. Apart from an infinitude of minor performances there is a fixed calendar of major festivals lasting nine days each. While there is a slight variation from year to year, the average amount of time devoted to religious ceremonial is one day in three. In the Hopi village of Walpi, for instance, the "year" starts with a nine-day initiation of youths into adult status. At the winter solstice there is a celebration in honor of the Kachina spirits, impersonated by mummers. In January the people play shinny as a magic fertility rite; moreover, several fraternities and sororities prepare the characteristic Pueblo offerings, such as feathered sticks to be smoked and prayed over before they are deposited in caves, springs, or other appropriate places. The Bean festival follows, with secret planting of the vegetable, distribution of beans and of seed corn, burlesques, masqueradings, and a legion of other ritualistic rites. After a period of spirit-impersonating dances, March ushers in the drama of the Water Snakes, with suckling of serpent images as part of a fertility ceremonial. In April, there is the first corn planting "for the Kachina"; in May, the Skeleton God is represented and ritualistically slain; in June, prayer-sticks must be made for the sun; in July, the Kachina spirits have their farewell ceremony. In August comes either of two festivals in regular alternation, the famous Snake Dance or the Flute Dance. In September and the early part of the fall the several feminine organizations perform, and in November youths are once more initiated.

Not all members of the community participate in the series in equal measure. Large portions of the esoteric rituals, the prerogative of special organizations, are barred to nonmembers; and within a fraternity the functions of the priest differ from those of the rank and file. However, even the outsider is affected by the solemnity that invests the community during the whole of a festival. Further, in a sense, everyone's welfare is involved, for whatever may be the special objects of major ceremonials, they are all meant to bring rain. As my interpreter quaintly put it, "The Hopi have no streams to irrigate with, so they must perform their ceremonies." These expert farmers who make a go of corn-growing where many White agriculturists would despair nevertheless believe unshakably in the indispensableness of ritual for gaining their ends. By wheedling the spirits, by mimicking whatever is associated with showers, they expect to wring rain from the powers of the universe. Now they offer their feathered sticks, now they draw pictures of clouds dropping precipitation, now they whirl a board through the air to simulate thunder.

The heavy display of fixed ritual in Hopi supernaturalism does not readily yield up its meaning from the worshipper's point of view. Literally thousands of pages in print about Pueblo ceremonies have until fairly recently left the reader almost wholly in the dark on this crucial point of the subject. As late as 1942 appeared Sun Chief's autobiography, which tells at least how one believer felt about it all.

Among the Plains Indians there was also some emphasis upon ritual, but it was overshadowed by the importance of the subjective thrill in visions, auditions, or particularly vivid dreams. The contrast between the Crow and the Hopi corresponds roughly to that popularly conceived between an established church and lay evangelism. However, if there were a ritual of however simple a nature it was observed with the same punctilio. I shall not readily forget the ceremonial opening of Flat-head-woman's sacred bundle. First he divided live embers into two heaps, strewed incense on both, then alternately lowered each end of the bundle toward the nearer heap. With muttered words of prayer he opened the bundle, its cloth wrappings being carefully folded back on the sides without disturbance of their relative positions. When possibly ten coverings had been gradually unfolded, nothing was visible but a large bunch of feathers. Flat-head-woman next combined the two heaps of embers, strewed more incense on top, then carefully arranged the feathers and extracted from among them, as the sacrosanct core, an arrow. This bundle was holy only because it had been revealed to the original owner (within Flat-head-woman's lifetime) by the Seven Stars. The arrow-spirit subsequently visited the first visionary's brother, Hillside, in his sleep. Hillside passed the bundle on to Flat-head-woman, who had never had a vision of his own; but after receiving the sacred bundle he began to have visions, seeing stalks of grass flying like arrows. For years he continued to receive revelations from the arrow-spirit. On one occasion it forbade him to throw ashes out of his lodge or to strike the lodge when removing snow from the tent cover. At another time it ordered him to visit the site of the original arrow revelation, where he was to find an eagle's feather in the cleft of a rock; and he found it.

The Crow, then, no less than the Hopi, attach extreme significance to things that we should regard as trivial. Both tribes insist upon a stereotyped procedure without the slightest deviation from the rules, lest you come to harm. Yet there is an immense difference between the tribes, for all those subjective experiences which are submerged in Hopi ritualism form the very warp and woof of Crow religion. The Crow Indians and their neighbors continually amazed me by their ever-recurring, face-to-face communication with the superhuman. It is such direct intercourse with the divine that is most distinctive of religion at its peak. As a veritable tyro I met Red-shirt, the Shoshone medicine-man who told me about his own death and resurrection. He had died, he said, because he had eaten salmon contrary to his familiar's orders and thus forever lost that spirit's protection. Fortunately, the Sun appeared to him in a dream, telling him he would die but promising resuscitation. This happened about 1880, and Red-shirt pointed out to me the spot where his tribesmen had built a special mortuary shelter for him. And now comes an illuminating detail. After his soul had stepped out of his thigh and taken a few steps forward, something suddenly descended clear through it, and it began to go downwards—not upwards, according to the general Shoshone belief. Red-shirt mistrusted the other Shoshone shamans no less than the Christian missionaries: Did he not have the direct evidence of his sense that the soul descended after death instead of rising? They were only guessing, but he *knew*. This adventure, though the most impressive in Red-shirt's career, was by no means the only one. Traveling at night on one occasion, he saw an Indian approaching; the face was invisible, but he was wearing a striped vest. As the figure got close, however, the stripes turned out to be bare ribs. Red-shirt fled from the specter, whom he headed off from pursuit by pronouncing a spell of exorcism: "You are only a ghost, leave me alone!" Then the figure wheeled about and vanished into the ground.

Selected Writings

This type of experience was reported to me wherever I went in the Northern Plains. The Stoney Assiniboine attached great importance to dreams. A man to whom a certain animal appeared in a dream would not kill or eat the flesh of its fellows. Only very young Stoneys dreamed of spirits, who would instruct them for several years and then depart for good. Jim Crack may be cited as an example: his benefactor, a dwarfish human, had taught him how to pursue every kind of game, so that Jim grew up to be a great hunter, after which his guide was seen no more. In Montana a blind Assiniboine recounted to me a series of personal revelations. Once he had been taken in a dream to a tent with a sun design on the cover; an old woman seated inside ordered him to decorate his own tent in the same manner and promised him that he and his family would enjoy good health. He did, and they did! On another occasion he received the right to doctor the sick. This was to be done in a special kind of painted tipi, the model being exhibited for his guidance; in it the practitioner was to be bound hand and foot and an invisible spirit would announce whether or not a cure was possible, and if so, would untie the doctor. Still another time my informant was shown a procession of Fool Dancers and bidden, on pain of premature death, to conduct their ceremony at least once a year. In 1908 he was still obeying this injunction, although total blindness had forced him to rely on the aid of a proxy.

It would be an exaggeration to say that every phase of a Crow's life was tinctured with religion, but it is literally true that every situation of strain or stress fused with the native concept of individual revelation. Thus, the young man who has been jilted goes off at once to fast in loneliness, praying for supernatural succor. An elk spirit may come and teach him a tune on a flute, as a means of luring the maiden back. The young man plays his tune, ensnares the haughty girl, and turns her away in disgrace, thus regaining his self-respect. Similarly, a wretched orphan who has been mocked by a young man of family hastens to the mountains to be blessed by some being, through whose favor he gains glory and loot on a raid, and can then turn the tables upon his tormentor. A woman big with child fasts and in a vision sees a weed which she subsequently harvests and through which she ensures a painless delivery. A gambler who has lost all his property retrieves his fortune through a revelation; and by the same technique a sorrowing kinsman identifies the slayers of his beloved relative and kills them. These are all typical instances, amply documented in personal recollections of informants and in traditional lore, showing the intrusion of religion into the frustrations of everyday living.

Out of this general atmosphere blossomed the notion that all conspicuous success in life is due to visions and revelations. Contrariwise, failure is interpreted as equivalent to lack of superhuman favor. As one informant put it: "All who had visions were well-to-do; I was to be poor, and that is why I had no visions." Such a man could still, however, tap hidden resources by borrowing a talisman—or a replica of one—from a more fortunate relative or friend. By its means he often managed to get a start, and later he might begin to have revelations of his own.

The question now arises as to how the ethnographer should appraise this faith in the reality, the paramount value, of visions. A casual estimate might suggest that the visionaries are all mystics or fools, but after several years' acquaintance with them, I am certain that they are neither. Every young man automatically went out to seek a vision, and those who claimed success were precisely the leaders of the tribe. The question still remains whether or not these men were intentional or unintentional frauds. My interpreter, a baptized Christian who was keenly aware of the inherent improbability by modern criteria of visions, thought otherwise. As he said, "When you listen to the old men telling their stories, you've just *got* to believe them." And in this impression I concur. Whatever the narrator's experiences may have been, he himself conceived them as being as he represented them.

But it is not necessary to rely upon subjective impressions, since there are at least four bits of evidence to suggest that the speakers were sincere. First, why should they lie to a white man, when they perfectly well knew that the more flamboyant their story the less likely I would be to believe it? Therefore, a pretense of wonderful experiences would serve no useful purpose for them. Second, among

Selected Writings

their own people, the rise to kudos through a vision required a good deal more than the palming off of a convenient hoax. Normally, the aspirant for a vision would go to the mountains, refrain for four days from food and water, and mutilate himself, to convince the deities of his sincerity. These offerings of flesh are not figments of myth, for I have seen the mutilated fingers and the deep scars on back and chest. Even with such austerities, there were many who never succeeded in getting a vision. I doubt that sheer mountebanks would lacerate or starve themselves. Third, even assuming that a man's desire for status drove him to self-mutilation and the fabrication of a dream or vision, he would be no better off than before, because it was only the *demonstrably successful* healer or war leader who achieved a following. Until the revelation was backed up with results, and unless it were, the would-be visionary was held up to endless ridicule. A deliberate imposter would, therefore, be far more likely to lose prestige than to gain it. And fourth, the man who received power through a revelation also received usually at least one and perhaps more life-long and onerous restrictions. One old man of my acquaintance had not ridden a horse since the day of his vision thirty years earlier, for the spirits had forbidden him to do so. He had trudged on foot. Although the ownership of horses had great prestige value, he had sold the one he owned at the time of his vision and had never owned another. He would gain military renown by killing an enemy but not by the much simpler method of stealing an enemy's horse. Another Indian had been forbidden to eat eggs and was a constant nuisance because he would not eat anything unless he personally supervised its preparation, lest the cook slip in an egg without his knowledge. And a third was forbidden to touch salmon, one of the Crow's few delicacies; on one occasion he ate a mixture of prepared fish without knowing there was salmon there and attributed the following eleven years of rheumatism to his unwitting breaking of his taboo. So a vision was not an unmixed blessing, and a man could hardly hope to derive benefit from a fake.

The role of religion in the life of either community or individual has already been at least implied. A living faith serves to integrate the individual's behavior in society, to give him confidence in meeting the crises which life inescapably brings, and to introduce into his existence a stable central core in the light of which he can assign values. These same purposes are served by the religion of those more sophisticated than my Indian informants, although they may not show the basis of their integration in so clear a fashion. Religion should also provide the basis for ethics. It should enter into everything an individual does, every judgment he makes, every point of view he develops. It is admittedly true that religion is not the only integrator; the impulse may come from immersion in art, music, education, or science in the case of those who have the necessary abilities for such absorption. For the average citizen, however, religion is still the most available source of integration. This fact not only justifies its existence but also explains its universal appeal.

Perhaps it might be well to take a momentary look at what has happened in modern times to societies that have deliberately set about exterminating religion, at least insofar as they could. The Nazis are a case in point. It did not take Hitler long to discover that the churches and the clergy were his implacable enemies. Priests and ministers insisted upon doing what they considered right, they criticized him openly, they tried to rally their congregations to oppose him, they helped enemies of the state to escape, they harbored the persecuted. Hitler could not put his policies of suppression, incarceration, and extermination into effect until he had eliminated the clergy, who would not do as they were told and would not keep their mouths shut. Moreover, they were upheld by a power that he did not understand but which he feared. During the ten years of his dominance the one effective resistance that he could not completely eliminate came from organized religion. One main purpose of his "youth" groups was to bring up a generation that lacked the Christian virtues of compassion or mercy. The soviets are attempting the same combination of repression and education of children without religious scruples. One *modus operandi* that has been used in totalitarian countries for the suppression of religion has been to carry away from each village as hostage one small child; thereafter, if any member of that village were caught at a secret religious gathering, if any gave aid to a member of the clergy, if any were seen saying his prayers, the child was killed. It is hard to imagine that in a country of even lukewarm Christianity such a method could be used. There are many people who might like to see the extermination of all religion, but perhaps they might take a closer look at what happens when religious attitudes are destroyed: the accompanying ethical standards also disappear, and one is left with a society not only without religion but also without restraining virtues. It is extremely doubtful that a nation can keep its ethics after it loses its religion.

For the last century at least much has been made of the conflict between religion and science and of the eventual and desirable substitution of the latter for the former. Perhaps before taking sides in this controversy one should consider to what extent the two systems of thought actually do contradict and interfere with each other. As soon as one stops to think, it is clear that there are vast bodies of scientific facts and principles that have never been challenged by any religious group—the ontogeny of silkworms, the expansion of mercury by heat, the predictability of an eclipse, the distance of the moon from the earth, the chemical constitution of water, the antiquity of man, the distinction between tame and domesticated animals, the germ theory of disease, the laws of gravity, and so on. In fact, the points upon which there is conflict are extremely few when compared to the sum total of scientific knowledge.

Perhaps the basic difficulty in seeing the relation of religion and science is that the majority of people do not know in the least what a science is, much less what it can and cannot do. The man-in-the-street commonly regards scientific facts as eternal truths—things that cannot change. Nothing could be more incorrect. To take a very simple example: in my chemistry class I was taught that an atom was an absolutely indivisible particle of matter, but now it seems that it is not; and the theory of light waves, as expounded to me in my college days, has long since been amended. And so on, in every field of science. The layman seems to think that because a scientific theory is derived from experiments it *must* be true; such a theory is true only until further experimentation shows wherein it must be altered. A theory is only a hypothesis that will have to do until a better one comes along. There is nothing fixed about it. Another misconception arises from the notion that science is independent of the social and economic pressures of the environment. Quite the reverse is true. Thus, the very problems that are attacked at a particular stage in history are selected by irrational considerations or outside economic pressures, rather than in the light of eternal fitness. This statement explains why classical Greece was so sterile in useful inventions. It was certainly not because of any dearth in acute thinkers or of any ineptitude for experimentation. The reason is to be sought rather in the predominant ideology, which exalted speculation over utilitarian application. Further, the social scheme allocated manual work to slaves, of which there was an ample supply. The tone-setting classes thus had no urge to minimize human effort by labor-saving devices. Those who were mechanically gifted accordingly lavished their ingenuity upon clever but useless toys, such as wooden pigeons that flew by compressed air.

Still another erroneous notion that one often hears expressed is the idea of the scientist as a person who dwells in an ivory tower, remote from the common pressures of mankind, and reaches his conclusions by the exercise of pure reason. This notion, made familiar by various forms of mass communication, is mostly poppycock, as may be shown by taking at random a few samples from the history of science. Ideally, of course, a scientist should be a man who is uniformly critical, willing to follow proof, and insistent upon the application of reason, but unfortunately he is a man like other men, with the same dependence upon tradition in his field, upon his own prejudices, upon his own social milieu. Thus we find Tycho Brahe, one of the foremost observational astronomers in the history of the science, piquing himself above all upon the accuracy not of his observations but of his horoscopes. History shows us again and again the whole guild of scientists rejecting epoch-making discoveries and advances that did not fit in with their traditional ideas. The scientists of his day branded Harvey as a charlatan for announcing his discoveries about the circulation of the blood, they martyrized Semmelweiss for expounding the cause of child-bed fever, they ridiculed Boucher de Perthes when he declared that man had been a contemporary of extinct annimals. These examples are taken from previous centuries, but the ability of a scientist to free himself from tradition and to embrace novel ideas has not increased greatly. Moreover, even a well-balanced, objective scientist is frequently mistaken in his conclusions, not because he does not reason but because he does not yet have all the facts he needs to reason with. Thus, a generation or two ago Lord Kelvin estimated the age of the earth at a figure absurdly low in the light of subsequent research.

To return to the original argument, there are of course points upon which science and religion collide, and the intensity of the clash naturally varies with the circumstances. Medical science is intransigent against religious cults that reject vaccination. Religious leaders may be equally determined to resist the principle of birth-control. Both sides have argued endlessly and to no great profit about Christian Science. Medical men have attacked it as being both useless and dangerous. Its defenders can point to much good that has been done for individuals. Probably both sides are right; they are simply talking about different people and different problems. If a man is a diabetic, he will not be cured by Christian Science, and the period during which he tries to effect a cure by such means may postpone medical treatment until it is too late to do much good. But if a man has a psychosomatic condition, he cannot be cured by a doctor's prescription because the sickness in his body is only a symptom of the sickness in his emotional life. There is a chance that Christian Science can cure him; there is no chance that a pill can. I am reminded of a cousin who was unemployed, depressed, and down to her last hundred dollars, of which she spent fifty for a "course" given by a complete charlatan who actually sent her nothing but form letters, all encouraging her to have faith in the future. Everyone, including myself, thought she was out of her mind, but we were all wrong because the man cured her. She returned to work and remained emotionally adjusted and useful throughout the remainder of her life. This sort of thing illustrates one point about human nature that is often not recognized: that what the average person wants is a workable solution, and he does not in the least care how many mistakes have been made in the computation.

There is thus no warrant for the notion that Science consists of a body of doctrine established once and for all time in the realm of Pure Reason. At any particular stage science is a sportsmanlike adventure in ferreting the truth out of a coy universe. And it is by no means the only method of approach. When we compare what is now known with what was known, say, four hundred years ago, there is every reason for good cheer. But even today research is not wholly a matter of earnest striving, specialized training, innate capacity for observation and deduction; it is the result of all these and of human frailty working under the handicap of a despotic heritage of traditional prejudice. The result is admittedly our best possible instrument for controlling physical environment and for formulating ideas of the material world. But it does not at all follow that it is soul-satisfying, or that it can serve as a basis for moral action.

If we keep before us the attitude of the man in the street, we shall understand why he can never be satisfied with science as a substitute for religion. That eternal striving for the truth without attaining it, which Lessing lauded as the highest good, has no appeal whatever for the generality of mankind. What the normal human being wants is peace, security, and relaxation. And he can never find these things in that dynamic, ever-growing, ever-disturbing thing that we have found science to be. In ringing words Ernst Mach has defined its nature: "The scientist's highest philosophy consists precisely in bearing an incomplete world-view and preferring it to one that is apparently complete, but inadequate." This is precisely the scientist's philosophy, but most people are nonscientists, and it is of them that I am speaking. The contrast is well expressed by Goethe's oft-quoted quatrain:

Wer Wissenschaft und Kunst besitzt
Hat auch Religion;
Wer jene beiden nicht besitzt,
Der habe Religion.

Whatever one may think of the snobbish flavor of these lines, they adumbrate an essential psychological truth. If a man's being is *wholly* absorbed in intellectual and esthetic pursuits, his interests may assume for him the place of spiritual guidance; without immersion in such activity, man had better rely upon the traditional faith. What an average man wants above everything else is security. But does science supply this? The answer is "No." That complete worldview that science explicitly renounces is precisely what the layman craves. In this perilous universe he is forever beset with dangers beyond his control. He wants at all odds to survive, and here science leaves him in the lurch—not everywhere and always, but often enough to make him keenly sensible of its imperfections. If he is dying of an incurable disease, it cheers him little to be told that medical science has made great strides in the past decades and that a remedy will almost certainly be found a hundred years hence, and probably sooner. Instead of running eagerly toward the latest scientific discovery, the average man is likely to wish the discovery had never been made, because it has proved so upsetting to his security. Science has achieved remarkable results, both practical and theoretical, but it has not made man a superman; so long as the enormous chasm yawns between man's rational control of nature and his biologico-psychological drives, there will still be room for belief in a Providence that grants not mere comfort, but security—not mere probability, but certainty. Religion and science thus perform different functions in the life of man, and it is not necessary that either should interfere with the other.

Bibliography

✣ *The following are works by Robert H. Lowie to which reference has been made in the text. For complete bibliographies of Lowie's publications, see Dundes (1966), Lowie (1959:181–98), and Radin (1958).*

1898   "Edgar Allan Poe," in *New Yorker Review*, Feb. 13.
1908   "The Test Theme in North American Mythology." *Journal of American Folklore* 21:97–148.
1909a "The Northern Shoshone." American Museum of Natural History, *Anthropological Papers* 2:165–302.
1909b "The Assiniboine." American Museum of Natural History, *Anthropological Papers* 4:1–270.
1909   With H. H. St. Clair. "Shoshone and Comanche Tales." *Journal of American Folklore* 22:3–20.
1914a "A Pro-German View." *The New Review* 2:642–44.
1914b "Some Recent Expressions on Racial Inferiority." *The New Review* 2:542–46.
1914c "Social Organization." *American Journal of Sociology* 20:68–97.
1915a "Exogamy and the Classificatory System of Relationship." *American Anthropologist* 17:223–39.
1915b "Exogamy and the Classificatory System of Relationship." *Proceedings of the National Academy of Sciences* 1:346–49.
1916   "Historical and Sociological Interpretation of Kinship Terminologies," in *Holmes Anniversary Volume*. Washington, D.C.

1917a *Culture and Ethnology.* New York: Douglas C. McMurtrie.
1917b "The Kinship Systems of the Crow and Hidatsa." *Nineteenth International Congress of Americanists,* pp. 340–43.
1920 *Primitive Society.* New York: Boni and Liveright.
1921 "The Eugenicist's Programme." *Freeman,* Oct. 19, pp. 129–130.
1924 *Primitive Religion.* New York: Boni and Liveright.
1927 *The Origin of the State.* New York: Harcourt Brace and Co.
1930 "A Crow Text with Grammatical Notes." *University of California Publications in American Archaeology and Ethnology* 29:155–75.
1934 *An Introduction to Cultural Anthropology.* New York: Farrar and Rinehart.
1936 "Lewis H. Morgan in Historical Perspective," in *Essays in Anthropology Presented to A. L. Kroeber* (R. Lowie, editor). Berkeley: University of California Press.
1937 *The History of Ethnological Theory.* New York: Farrar and Rinehart.
1940 "Native Languages as Ethnographic Tools." *American Anthropologist* 42:81–89.
1942 "The Crow Language; Grammatical Sketch and Analyzed Text." *University of California Publications in American Archaeology and Ethnology* 39:1–142.
1943 "Property Rights and Coercive Powers of Plains Indian Military Societies." *Journal of Legal and Political Sociology* 1:59–71.
1945 *The German People: A Social Portrait to 1945.* New York: Farrar and Rinehart.
1946 "Evolution in Cultural Anthropology: A Reply to Leslie White." *American Anthropologist* 48:223–33.
1947 "Franz Boas, 1858–1942." National Academy of Sciences, *Biographical Memoirs* 24:303–20.
1948a *Social Organization.* New York: Rinehart and Co.
1948b *Primitive Religion* (revised edition), New York: Liveright Publishing Co.
1951 "Some problems of Geographical Distribution." *Südseestudien.* Basel: Museum für Völkerkunde, pp. 11–26.
1954 *Toward Understanding Germany.* Chicago: University of Chicago Press.
1959 *Robert H. Lowie, Ethnologist: A Personal Record.* Berkeley and Los Angeles: University of California Press.
1960 "Empathy, or Seeing from Within," in *Culture and History: Essays in Honor of Paul Radin* (S. Diamond, editor). New York: Columbia University Press.

✤ *References to works by other authors*

Benedict, Ruth
 1946 *The Chrysanthemum and the Sword.* Boston: Houghton Mifflin.

Robert H. Lowie

Du Bois, Cora (editor)
    1960 *Lowie's Selected Papers in Anthropology.* Berkeley and Los Angeles: University of California Press.
    1971 Personal communication.

Dundes, Alan
    1966 *The Complete Bibliography of Robert H. Lowie.* Berkeley: The Robert H. Lowie Museum of Anthropology.

Durkheim, Emile
    1915 *The Elementary Forms of the Religious Life.* London: George Allen & Unwin. (Originally published in 1912.)

Engels, F.
    1942 *Origin of the Family, Private Property and the State.* New York: International Publishers. (Originally published in 1884.)

Fried, Morton
    1967 *The Evolution of Political Society.* New York: Random House.

Harris, Marvin
    1968 *The Rise of Anthropological Theory.* New York: Thomas Y. Crowell Co.

Kroeber, Alfred L.
    1909 "Classificatory Systems of Relationship." *Journal of the Royal Anthropological Institute* 39:77–84.

Lévi-Strauss, Claude
    1963 *Tristes Tropiques.* New York: Atheneum. (Originally published in 1955.)

Maine, Henry S.
    1861 *Ancient Law.* London: J. Murray.

McLennan, J. F.
    1865 *Primitive Marriage.* Edinburgh: Adams and Charles Black.

Mead, Margaret
    1939 "Native Languages as Fieldwork Tools." *American Anthropologist* 41:189–203.

Morgan, Lewis Henry
    1871 *Systems of Consanguinity and Affinity of the Human Family.* Washington, D.C.: Smithsonian Contributions to Knowledge XVII.
    1877 *Ancient Society.* New York: World Publishing.

Murphy, Robert F.
    1956 "Matrilocality and Patrilineality in Mundurucú Society." *American Anthropologist* 58:414–34.
    1958 "Mundurucú Religion." *University of California Publications in American Archaeology and Ethnology* 49, no. 1. Berkeley and Los Angeles: University of California Press.

Radcliffe-Brown, A. R.
    1952 "The Study of Kinship Systems." (Originally published in 1941), in *Structure and Function in Primitive Society.* Glencoe, Ill.: The Free Press.

Radin, Paul
    1958   "Robert H. Lowie; 1883–1957." *American Anthropologist* 60:358–75.
Rivers, W. H. R.
    1907   "On the Origin of the Classificatory System of Relationships," in *Anthropological Essays Presented to Edward Burnett Tylor*. Oxford: Oxford University Press.
    1914   *Kinship and Social Organization*. London: Constable.
Sahlins, Marshall, and Elman Service
    1960   *Evolution and Culture*. Ann Arbor: University of Michigan Press.
Schurtz, Heinrich
    1902   *Alterklassen und Männerbünde*. Berlin: Reimer.
Steward, Julian H.
    1938   "Basin-Plateau Sociopolitical Groups." *Bureau of American Ethnology Bull.* 120, Washington, D.C.
    1946–   "Handbook of South American Indians," 6 vols., *Bureau of American Ethnology*
    1950   *Bull.* 143, Washington, D.C.
    1955   *Theory of Culture Change*. Urbana: University of Illinois Press.
Tylor, Edward B.
    1865   *Researches into the Early History of Mankind and the Development of Civilization*. London: J. Murray.
    1889   "On a Method of Investigating the Development of Institutions; Applied to Laws of Marriage and Descent." *Journal of the Royal Anthropological Institute* 18: 245–69.
    1896   "The Matrilineal Family System." *Nineteenth Century* XL:81–96.